THE
ADEPT
CHURCH

F. Douglas Powe, Jr.

THE ADEPT CHURCH

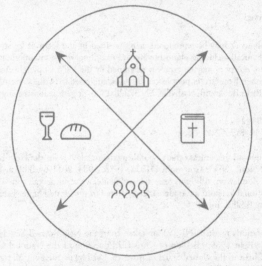

Navigating Between a Rock and a Hard Place

Abingdon Press

Nashville

THE ADEPT CHURCH:
NAVIGATING BETWEEN A ROCK AND A HARD PLACE

Copyright © 2020 by Abingdon Press

LCCN: 2019954249
ISBN: 978-1-5018-9652-1

20 21 22 23 24 25 26 27 28 29—10 9 8 7 6 5 4 3 2 1
MANUFACTURED IN THE UNITED STATES OF AMERICA

I am dedicating this book to all the students who I have taught over the years. I am grateful for all that they have taught and shared with me.

CONTENTS

ACKNOWLEDGMENTS

I am grateful for the careful and hard work by Ann Michel and Carol Follett on this book. Without the superb editing by the two of them, this book would not be possible.

INTRODUCTION

*For if you remain silent at this time, relief and deliverance for
the Jews will arise from another place, but you and your father's
family will perish. And who knows but that you have come to
your royal position for such a time as this?*
—Esther 4:14

Imagine being a young girl and learning from the cousin who
raised you that your ethnic community is going to be annihi-
lated. The one person who can stop the annihilation is the king.
You just happen to be a part of the royal harem. But, unfortunately, the king has not called you into his presence for thirty
days. If you try to see the king without being called, it could
mean your death. You are straddling the horns of a dilemma. On
the one side is the fate of your entire community. On the other
side is the risk to your own life should you attempt to influence
the one person who can stop it. You can easily understand how
Esther feels trapped between a rock and a hard place. Neither
choice seems like a good option, and either choice could lead to
her death.

Many of us have experienced at some point in our lives the
feeling of being trapped between a rock and hard place—the
horrible fate of facing a losing proposition no matter which

direction we turn. Esther certainly must have felt trapped by circumstances as she confronted the choice between the destruction of her community and the risk to her own life. Reading between the lines of the story, we can imagine the wheels turning in her mind. She wonders if maybe, just maybe, she is immune from the decree. She contemplates for a moment that as a member of the royal harem she is safe. Perhaps she can somehow avoid making the hard choice. Could the status quo be working in her favor?

In Esther 4:13-14, Mordecai brings her back to reality. He reminds her that she is in the same boat as the rest of her community. She is not immune from the forthcoming destruction. In fact, he says, "Who knows but that you have come to your royal position for such a time as this?" But let's be honest. It's easy for Mordecai to talk this way when it's not his life on the line. Esther is the one stuck between the rock and the hard place. Yes, Mordecai faces annihilation, but he is not putting his life on the line by going to see the king.

In 4:15, Esther begins to perceive her dilemma differently. The circumstances do not change, but the way she sees the circumstances changes. She has been in a reactive posture up to this point in the story, but now she begins to recognize her own agency. Esther discovers that even amidst these adverse choices there is a possibility for moving ahead boldly. Realizing that to rescue herself and her community she needs to think outside the box, she comes to embody "for such a time as this" in ways that Mordecai probably never imagined.

Esther instructs Mordecai and others in her community to fast for three days and nights. Then she states that she and her attendants will do the same. This time of fasting leads to the development of her plan to reverse fate. Esther does not dwell on being stuck in troubling circumstances but on shaping a new future.

You may be saying, "Sure, this is a heartwarming Bible story, but what does it have to do with my church?" I believe Esther's capacity for innovative and creative leadership, even when stuck between a rock and a hard place, should capture our attention. Many congregations today are stuck between a rock and a hard place. On the one hand, they are declining at a rate moving them rapidly toward extinction. On the other hand, the culture is shifting in a direction that seems hostile to renewed congregational vitality.

This shifting cultural landscape befuddles many congregations. They keep waiting for a return to the status quo. They cling to the outdated assumption that people will naturally be attracted to the church just because they have been attracted to it in the past. But the reality today is that even people who claim to be spiritual are not necessarily attracted to the church, as evidenced by the continual rise of the "nones"—people who respond "none" when asked to identify their religious affiliation. Today, almost 23 percent of Americans fall into this category.[1] Yet most congregations continue to operate as if nothing has changed. They persist in assuming that individuals not coming to church are still somehow interested in church.

Our movie-watching habits provide a helpful analogy. There was a time when Blockbuster ruled the movie rental business. Blockbuster opened stores in most US cities and experienced rapid growth. New players came on the scene, such as Redbox and Netflix, altering the movie rental delivery system. Blockbuster continued to work with a mindset that people wanted to come to their brick-and-mortar stores. Blockbuster is no longer in business because it held on to that outmoded mindset.

Many congregations will suffer the same fate as Blockbuster if they ignore cultural change and continue to hold a mindset based on old assumptions. They are between a rock and a hard place, trapped between the reality of congregational decline and shifting cultural currents. And worse than just being stuck in place, they are caught in a downward spiral. The more a congregation declines, the more they cling to the old reality. A rock and a hard place.

It's not just congregations that are caught in this trap. Their leaders are trapped as well. On the one hand, they want things to run smoothly without having to upset the applecart. They seek congregational stability. On the other hand, these same leaders are pressured, often by denominational leaders, to increase vitality, which requires upsetting the applecart. These leaders are stuck between choosing to keep things going in order to maintain some semblance of stability or upsetting the applecart and having the whole thing fall apart. A rock and a hard place.

Like Esther in that brief moment, believing that doing nothing made her safe, these congregational leaders hope they can simply maintain the status quo and avoid having to make the changes necessary to revitalize. But merely maintaining stability is no guarantee of long-term survival. Mordecai's words, "Do not think you are exempt from what is taking place," should echo in their ears. But often no one is giving voice to such a warning. Or leaders choose to ignore it.

While congregations and congregational leaders must acknowledge the reality of their circumstances, they do not have to wallow in it. Esther knew the odds were not in her favor. Yet she decided to act boldly rather than wait for fate to take its course. Being stuck between a rock and a hard place is scary, uncomfortable, and overwhelming. Yet it is a place where we have the opportunity to try God-sized experiments, where we can set aside our preoccupation with the status quo and innovate. Is it possible that you, like Esther, have been called to "such a time as this"? Is this the time to take a risk, to upset the applecart, knowing that it could lead either to destruction or to something new and wonderful?

A *missional* mindset is required to take such a bold stance. To be missional is to focus on God inviting us into the ongoing work of transforming the world. This transformational work is practical, spiritual, and directed toward something new.

- Missional transformation is **practical** because it requires us to feed the hungry and journey with individuals trying to carve out a sense of meaning for their lives.

- Missional transformation is **spiritual** because it commits us to following Jesus in ways that make us comfortable and uncomfortable.

- Missional transformation is **directed toward something new** because we as a body of believers create a community that is different from what has been experienced in other places.

This is the work that Jesus did during his time on earth. It is the work to which we are called. The challenge is embracing all three aspects of a missional orientation, not just one or two. Many congregations pick one or maybe two and are satisfied that they are fulfilling the gospel. Being missional requires that we do all three, even when our culture pushes against creating a community that cares for the body, soul, and mind of individuals.

Understanding what it means to be missional in this way sheds new light on our task as leaders and on our congregational circumstances. It allows us to reimagine how and where God is calling us. Pursuing God's call "for such a time as this" requires that we reevaluate the way in which we *adopt*, *adapt*, and are *adept* at pursuing that call.

- We must learn to **adopt** practices that are life-giving and not life-draining. For instance, it is typically life-draining to simply adopt the latest trends and add them to worship or Bible study and hope for a miracle. Simply seeking more financial and human resources will not help us recreate the ministries of the megachurch down the street. We must learn to adopt life-giving practices instead of just jumping on the bandwagon of the latest fad.

- We must learn to **adapt** in helpful ways, ideas, or practices that promote fruitfulness. Often, leaders will read or hear about something that works great in another congregation or context. They try to adapt the idea to their own congregation. But without careful consideration of the contextual implications, the new idea or practice may detract from their mission more than it adds to it. Successful adaptation of new ideas and practices requires that we understand both the idea and the contextual factors influencing how it can best be adapted to our setting.

- We must learn to **be adept** by creating something new while still maintaining the original intent of our ministry. Jesus was adept in this way. He knew how to adopt and adapt ideas in a way that created something new, while honoring the original intent from which it came. This is discussed in detail in chapter 2, but the key point is that leadership requires more than just adopting and adapting things. It requires decision making that is innovative and builds bridges between what came before and the new ideas being brought forth.

In congregations today, the primary challenge is to help leaders become more adept at making the decisions that will help them to build those bridges, even when it doesn't make everyone happy. There were plenty of naysayers during Jesus's time who thought he was destroying the faith as they understood it. They were not willing to change or let go of the past in any form or fashion. In Luke 13:10-17, we read about the synagogue leader who was upset that, on the Sabbath, Jesus healed a woman crippled for eighteen years. To that synagogue leader, Jesus was breaking a commandment and violating the faith. But Jesus perceived it as returning the woman to community so she could go the temple and uphold the faith.

Like the synagogue leader, we misjudge the mission today when we uphold traditions at the expense of connecting people to the community. The person seeking to move the Easter egg hunt from the church grounds to a neighborhood park is a heretic for going against the tradition. We fail to see that when people look for new ways to be faithful and offer new insights, they may be building upon past traditions and ideas.

This book seeks to help leaders and congregations become more adept at moving forward in a bold manner. This requires precision in both thought and action. We do not have the luxury of merely coming up with the right ideas that will never be put into action. Nor do we have the luxury of rushing to action before fully thinking through the missional implications of what we propose. For leaders and congregations to avoid being stuck between a rock and a hard place, they must move forward with new vitality and vision. They must truly believe that they have been called "for such a time as this."

SWAMP, RESERVOIR, OR CANAL

Are you a reservoir or are you a canal or a swamp?
—Howard Thurman

"A re you a reservoir or are you a canal or a swamp?"[1] Howard Thurman posed this question in relation to our personal lives. He believed our personal lives can take on the characteristics of these bodies of water. And knowing which best describes us gives insight into our journey.

I believe the question is relevant to congregations as well. "Is your congregation a swamp, reservoir, or canal?" Some congregations may display traits of all three while exhibiting the dominant characteristics of one. Naming this aspect of a church's existence helps determine how it can best move forward.

Swamp

Thurman describes a swamp as a place that hoards, is friendless, and where things decay.[2] Writing at a time that predates our modern understanding of a swamp as a complex, living ecosystem, Thurman draws on the popular parlance of his day to describes a swamp as a scary place that swallows life. Swamps are often depicted this way in movies. The swamp is a dreary, lonely place that emits strange, eerie sounds. We imagine that things go into the swamp, but they do not come back out.

Applying Thurman's definition of swamp to congregations, a swamp church is one that hoards, is friendless (or only inwardly friendly), and where things decay. Hoarding can be loosely defined as stashing, keeping, and guarding things so that no one else can take them. Typically, hoarders are unwilling to let anything go. They seek to keep things from others. They guard their stash so no one can get it. A hoarding church is unwilling to share their resources or themselves with others. They instinctively guard what they have because they fear that letting go of anything will hasten their demise. They hold on for dear life to what they have out of fear of a bleak future.

Thurman describes the water in a swamp as having no outlet.[3] Again, while Thurman may not have understood the ecosystem completely, he is describing a self-contained, inwardly focused system. The water in a swamp does not connect with other bodies of water. A swamp congregation is self-contained and seeks nothing outside of itself. They are happy with the way things are currently. Their idea of change is to add a few more folks like the ones they already have and keep going just as they are. Folks who do not fit their swamp-like characteristics will not feel welcome. There is little interest in reaching out beyond themselves. All connecting is done inside the church. The church is inwardly focused.

Thurman also observes that a swamp is where things go to decay.[4] To decay is to rot slowly over time until ultimately there is nothing left. But it can take a long time for some things to decay. Congregations that hoard and are not connecting with others are decaying. Ultimately, these congregations will cease to exist, but the decomposition can take a long, long time. A church with an endowment can go on for years even though it is decaying daily. Congregations in this state typically think the problem lies with others, not with themselves. They are slowly decaying but place the blame on everything around them.

If your congregation is like a swamp, it hoards all forms of resources. It does not seek to connect with outsiders. It is decaying slowly. Ultimately, the congregation will die, even if it is a slow and lengthy death. A swamp congregation exists merely to survive, helping a little here or there, but lacking a clear missional focus. Any congregation can have certain ministries or programs that are swamp-like. But the real concern is when this is the dominant characteristic of the whole church. And the truth is, far too many congregations today are swamp congregations.

Reservoir

Thurman says a reservoir "is a place in which water is stored in order that it may be available when needed."[5] A reservoir is a storehouse for supplies. It is a place where one can go and get something that is needed. Many of us have driven by or seen pictures of reservoirs that store water for a city or town. The reservoir is a source of comfort because the community knows it has adequate water in reserve. If the water supply in the reservoir runs low, it is cause for concern or even fear. A reservoir assures that water is available when needed, so it is important

3

that the water supply does not diminish to a point where the reservoir may run dry.

Reservoir churches are perceived as places that have resources. These congregations often focus on providing material resources to those in their community. They are involved in feeding ministry, clothing ministry, and so on. Unlike swamp congregations, they seek to connect with those outside the congregation. In most cases, they are more vital than swamp congregations because they are not entirely inwardly focused.

However, a reservoir congregation still faces challenges. While outwardly focused, that outward focus tends to take the shape of a pet ministry. For example, a strong feeding ministry is the primary point of connection with those beyond the congregation, but there is little effort to connect in other ways. If a person outside the congregation does not participate in the feeding ministry, it is unlikely she will ever come in contact with someone from the church. In some cases, even those who participate in the feeding ministry quickly figure out the congregation is happy to give them food but is uninterested in building relationships. The congregation may pray with the people they help, but the goal is not to help them to become disciples. It is simply to provide goods or services. The congregation operates more like a social service agency with repeat clients. It is still inwardly focused in that it perceives its worship life as separate from its outreach.

A key difference between a swamp congregation and a reservoir congregation is the intentional way in which resources are shared. But reservoir congregations can be at risk of developing a hoarder mentality. If they start seeing fewer resources coming in, they are tempted to start restricting the amount going out. The congregation may view this as good stewardship, not hoarding. But when more and more is left in the storehouse and less and less is shared, the ministry starts to suffer and eventually decay because the church has taken on a swamp mentality. Reservoir congregations walk a fine line between putting things in reserve for the future and hoarding reserves in a way that will kill the ministry.

Thurman remarks that the inflow and outflow of a reservoir must be maintained well.[6] What keeps a reservoir vital is maintaining the proper balance between what it takes in and what it gives out. For a congregation, the goal is to make sure an inwardly focused mentality does not dominate the approach to ministry. Unless a reservoir congregation stays outwardly focused, it will become a swamp.

Reservoir congregations have the potential to build on their ministry efforts and seek other ways of connecting outside of the congregation. But they typically resist this because it is perceived as a drain on financial or human resources. Reservoir congregations teeter toward stagnation when they are unwilling to move beyond a superficial level of outreach. The good news is, the congregation is getting outside its doors and reaching others. The bad news is, the outreach often is not focused on discipleship.

If your congregation is a reservoir church, it exhibits the traits of a social service agency and fails to focus intentionally on discipleship. The congregation is outwardly focused in terms of helping others, but often worries about running out of resources. Reservoir congregations are more vital than swamp congregations, but they can take on a swamp mentality if they are not careful. These congregations are at risk of taking a step backward if they do not move forward with boldness.

5

Canal

Thurman wrote that "the function of a canal is to channel water"—it helps water flow or move from place to place.[7] He describes a canal as a connector. It is a body of water linked to things outside of itself.[8] Imagine a canal congregation as a body that links to things outside of itself. It is outwardly focused because it is always looking to connect to things beyond its origin.

A canal congregation knows its transforming power is in the ability to move away from its center and not remain stagnant in one place. It seeks to touch others in the community and get them engaged in discipleship. A canal congregation realizes this may not always happen inside the church building. It seeks to reach people where they are and impact their lives. This may take the shape of ministries addressing people's physical and material needs while also sharing with them the power of being a disciple. It may involve trying a new form of worship that connects with individuals who are not a part of the congregation. A canal congregation is always looking outside of itself rather than simply trying to attract people to come to it.

The beauty of a canal is that its fundamental purpose is relational. It exists not for its own sake but for the sake of linking together things that are in its path. Canal congregations do ministry for people but are intentional about involving them in building something that includes discipleship. Canal congregations see resources as a means of enabling better connections for missional purposes. They do not hoard resources or operate like social service agencies. They share resources all along the way and move them to where they can be of most use. As long as the canal congregation stays true to its fundamental purpose, it can avoid an insider mentality. But if the congregation ceases to be a place that connects to things outside of itself, it risks slipping into hoarding or a social services mindset.

The dominant characteristic of only a very few congregations is that of a canal. Some of the ministries or missional efforts of a church may have canal traits, but it is rare for the whole congregation to be a canal. To be a canal, a congregation must dedicate its life to being relational like Jesus. Most congregations do this in bits and spurts or in particular areas of ministry. But it is rare for a congregation to commit itself completely to being a canal.

The challenge of being a canal congregation is a willingness to always be a connector—connecting with people outside of the church and connecting people inside and outside the church to Jesus. The work of connecting never ends and requires a constant channeling of resources. It is not dependent on the size of the congregation, but it depends rather on the congregation's level of commitment. If a canal congregation is not vigilant in maintaining an outward focus, it runs the risk of becoming a social service agency or a hoarding congregation.

If your congregation is like a canal, it is constantly connecting to others outside of itself. It is always looking to expand its network of relationships, while maintaining the network already in place. We need more canal congregations, but the reality is it requires a high commitment.

Sober Judgment

Is your congregation a swamp, reservoir, or canal? This is the question that all congregations need to ask and answer honestly. Paul writes in Romans, "For by the grace given me I say to every one of you: Do not think of yourself more highly than you ought, but rather think of yourself with sober judgment, in accordance with the faith that God has distributed to each of you" (Rom 12:3). These words remind us of the need to take a hard look in the mirror and be honest in appraising ourselves. We need to avoid the tendency to see all the good and think too highly of ourselves or to see all the bad and devalue ourselves. The goal is to use sober judgment and see ourselves as we truly are.

Thinking Too Highly of Yourself

The tendency in some struggling congregations is to overlook those areas where things are not going well. Think of the analogy of how we approach year-end job evaluations. When asked to evaluate our job performance, we tend to find ways to rank ourselves highly in every category. This is not necessarily a deliberate effort to pump ourselves up. But each of us tends to see things in a way that is slanted to maintain our favorable self-perception. For example, if I am a sales representative and I did not make my goal, I may still justify giving myself a strong evaluation by taking into consideration some of the reasons I did not make my goal. Perhaps another company started selling a more competitive product. It's not that I failed to do my part, but the circumstances were beyond my control. We easily find all kinds of explanations for our failure. And they can be 100 percent accurate. But it doesn't change the reality of the current situation when we take an honest look in the mirror. Similarly, congregations can think of all kinds of reasons why things are not going well for them. And all the reasons may be valid. But it does not alter the image of their current reality when they look honestly in the mirror.

Every addiction treatment or recovery program begins with an honest admission of the addict's current situation. Many congregations are swamps, but it is challenging for them to admit it. They need to look in the mirror and be honest with themselves. Any hope of altering the situation has to begin with an honest assessment.

Here are some key questions in a process of honest self-appraisal to aid a congregation that tends to think too highly of itself:

How many visitors do you see on average in a month?

How are you modeling for those inside the congregation what it means to be to imitators of Jesus?

How are you modeling for those outside the congregation what it means to be imitators of Jesus?

How many visitors return a second time or continue coming?

How many people do you connect with in the community during the month?

How are these community connections happening?

Are these connections based on giving out food, clothing, and so on? This list is not meant to be comprehensive, but to help you take a serious look in the mirror. If you are not seeing visitors or they do not come back, that should raise a red flag. If you are making no community connections or the connections simply exist to hand out goods, that should raise a red flag. If you are only being imitators of Jesus inside the congregation, that should raise a red flag. Reread the description of swamp, reservoir, and canal congregations after answering these questions. What do you see in the mirror?

Thinking Too Lowly of Yourself

Alternatively, some struggling congregations are prone to thinking too lowly of themselves. They pick on every single thing they do to the point of talking themselves out of a good thing. Returning to the analogy of a year-end job evaluation, they are like the person who scores themselves low on most things because they feel they do not measure up. The person always perceives something is lacking and that others are better suited for the job. It can lead to low self-esteem. A congregation with low self-esteem can lose hope and begin to live out a self-fulling prophecy. The congregation starts to say things like, "We can never be as good as that congregation down the street." They get trapped in a game of comparing themselves to other congregations and feeling as if they continually come up short.

Here are some key questions to aid in a process of honest self-appraisal for a congregation prone to thinking too lowly of itself:

Do we feel as if we have to keep up with other congregations?

Are we frustrated by the participation numbers when we start something new?

Are we frustrated with the pace that things are changing?

This is not a complete list, but it will help you to determine where you may be so hard on yourself that you are becoming paralyzed. Heightened frustration with keeping up with other congregations and the pace of change should raise a red flag.

Whether a congregation thinks too highly or too lowly of itself, the danger is the same. In either case, a failure to view its situation objectively leads to paralysis. Neither congregation will do what is needed to restore vitality. Paul's admonition to exercise sober judgment is a good one, and we should take it to heart. Congregations need to look in the mirror and be honest about who they are. This means thinking neither too highly nor too lowly of themselves because both can leave a congregation mired in the swamp. Only when we are honest with ourselves are we in a position to start changing.

While congregations can take on a life of their own, they are also influenced by those in leadership. The pastor and key lay leaders will influence the way a congregation perceives its reality and what can be done about it. Leadership is discussed in depth later in this book, but with regard to assessing their circumstances, leaders have two key roles.

First, leaders must look in the mirror and hold the mirror for others. As leaders look into the mirror themselves, they must exercise sober judgment and be honest about their own role in a congregation. For instance, some leaders resist change. They seek to maintain the status quo because they don't want to rock the boat. Other leaders seek such sweeping changes that everyone may be left disillusioned and questioning why they chose to become followers of Jesus. Leaders must find a way to move people forward while helping them to stay in love with Jesus. This is not an easy task. But it is a critical one.

Leaders must also hold the mirror up for others in the congregation to see themselves. The leaders may need to encourage and even cajole those in the congregation to look in the mirror—to appraise themselves and their church honestly. This is not an easy task because we so often want to avoid seeing the truth. But only when we expose ourselves to the truth can we begin to move forward in a determined way.

Second, leaders must be intentional about the way they imitate Jesus. This gets at the heart of discipleship and that which we are called to do. Leaders help others to live missional lives that invite them into a pattern of discipleship. Leaders must model this pattern so that others will be able to see it. Jesus did not simply tell the disciples what to do. Jesus modeled for them a life of prayer, healing, worshipping, listening, and acting. The disciples were able to lead because they witnessed Jesus doing it. And then they went out and modeled it for others.

Between a Rock and a Hard Place

Whether a congregation is a swamp, reservoir, or canal, it can be trapped between a rock and a hard place. Swamp congregations are caught in the tension between the risk of extinction and the hope of becoming a reservoir congregation. Reservoir congregations exist between falling back to a swamp or becoming a canal congregation. Canal congregations exist between falling back to a reservoir and trying to stay a canal congregation. This reality shapes many congregations as they try to figure out how to be vital in a changing culture.

Just as so many congregations are between a rock and a hard place, so too are their leaders. They are caught between just going along to keep everyone happy and upsetting the apple-cart in an attempt to become something new. To lead effectively, they must constantly navigate between these two choices. Leaders who give in to one or the other will look in the mirror one day and see that they have landed the congregation in the swamp. To steer clear of this trap, leaders must constantly examine themselves, while holding the mirror up to others as well. And they must be intentional about how they imitate Jesus. The next chapter explores the role that leaders play in helping congregations to be adept in making decisions.

ESTHER INTERLUDE ONE

Hathak went back and reported to Esther what Mordecai had said. Then she instructed him to say to Mordecai, "All the king's officials and the people of the royal provinces know that for any man or woman who approaches the king in the inner court without being summoned the king has but one law: that they be put to death unless the king extends the gold scepter to them and spares their lives. But thirty days have passed since I was called to go to the king."

—Esther 4:9-11

Let's briefly revisit Esther's story. Esther hears about her cousin Mordecai in sackcloth at the king's gate. Her first response is to send clothes. This response is interesting because it is a way of avoiding the real issue. Growing up in the Jewish culture, Esther would have known Mordecai's behavior was a form of mourning. Yet she does not ask Mordecai why he mourns. She responds by simply sending clothes—a response that avoids dealing with the real issue.

How many congregations fall into a similar trap? The real issue is decline, but we focus instead on addressing financial challenges. We deflect attention from the real issue at stake by looking for other ways to paper over problems. Like Esther, we are more interested in window dressing, in covering things over, than in seeing the truth of the situation. We hope the core problem will simply go away. We avoid taking the hard look in the mirror discussed in chapter 1. This type of avoidance is characteristic of swamp congregations. And if reservoir and canal congregations are not careful, a pattern of avoidance can start their descent into the swamp as well.

While most of us do not like confronting uncomfortable situations or unpleasant individuals, the truth of the matter is, avoidance only postpones the inevitable. At some point, we have to deal with the real issue. It is hard work, but necessary work. Esther finally sends Hathak to find out what is disturbing Mordecai. Mordecai shares the king's edict calling for the destruction of the Jews. He beseeches Esther to go to the king and try to persuade him against it. Hathak reports all this back to Esther.

Esther's initial response is grounded in her instinct for self-preservation. Approaching the king without being summoned would put her in great danger. It is easy to criticize Esther at this point in the story for a lack of courage. But it bears repeating that Mordecai is not putting his life on the line, so we should not be too harsh on Esther. She realizes her very life is at risk if she moves forward with the plan of seeing the king. She can avoid that risk by not going to see the king. Her response is understandable. It is the one most of us would give under similar circumstances.

In this story, we see how risk avoidance can overtake decision-making in our personal lives, and it is doubly so for congregations. Learning to embrace a certain amount of risk is hard.

Most congregations instinctively seek to avoid risk. They want to play it safe. They don't want to deal with the real issues at stake. They reject any plan that requires putting themselves in a vulnerable position. They turn in on themselves in an attempt to protect themselves from potential loss or harm. It is perceived to be an act of self-preservation. Typically, such congregations are not purposely making decisions out of self-interest. But by avoiding the real issue and shielding themselves from vulnerability, they end up making self-interested decisions that create a downward spiral landing them in the swamp.

Mordecai counters Esther's response by pointing out that just because she is safe in the moment does not mean she will always be safe. Esther hears this and decides to act boldly. She is willing to take the risk even though she is unsure of the outcome. This is not risk-taking for its own sake but taking a risk for the sake of a larger purpose. Esther steps forward because the life of her nation is at stake.

Is your congregation willing to do the same? Being outwardly focused requires a willingness to take risks even when we cannot see the outcome. It is risk-taking done with purpose— a missional purpose. The goal is to live out the calling God has placed upon us. There is no better or clearer purpose for any congregation to undertake. We must focus on God, not on self-preservation. The more a congregation focuses on self-preservation the more likely it is to take on swamp characteristics. Conversely, the more a congregation risks bold actions the more likely it is to become a reservoir or canal. As Jesus taught, the ironic truth is "those who want to save their life will lose it, and those who lose their life for my sake will find it" (Matt 16:25 NRSV).

Our decisions and practices shape the type of congregation we are and will become. We need to face these decisions honestly and think through all the ramifications. Like Esther, we need to be creative and brave enough to move out of our comfort zones. The next chapter explores a way of approaching these critical decisions in a way that creates a missional culture.

Chapter Two

ADEPT CONGREGATION

I f I asked most congregations the following three questions the answers would be "Yes," "Maybe," and "No." Question 1: "Do you want to be missional?" Most congregations will reply "Yes." Even if they are unsure what it really means to be missional, it sounds like something they should want to be. Question 2: "Are you willing to change in order to be missional?" The truthful response for most is "No." But many will find a way to hem and haw and avoid answering "Yes" or "No." It comes down to "Maybe," depending on what change is required. Question 3: "Do you know what is required to be missional?" Typically, you get answers like, "I remember my pastor using the word *missional*." The bottom line for this answer is "No." Most people have no clue what is required.

Most congregations want to be missional, but the truth is they have no idea how to do so. To further complicate matters, many congregations are unwilling to change until things get beyond desperate. If most congregations want to be missional, what stands in their way? I believe the answer may lie in how these congregations approach decision making.

The way congregations have made decisions and are continuing to make decisions greatly determines if they are swamps, reservoirs, or canals. Canal congregations are making more

19

missionally focused decisions; meanwhile, swamp congregations are making decisions focused on self-interest or survival. It is important for congregations to consider how they are currently making decisions and a process for doing it better.

Consider our personal lives. Decisions are not made in a vacuum. We all have a framework that informs our decision making. That framework is shaped by many factors, such as geographical location, education, ethnicity, and so on. All these factors play a role in how we make everyday decisions. For instance, an individual born in Ohio will likely decide to be an Ohio State fan rather than a Michigan fan due to influences connected with their geographical location. In Ohio, surrounded by Ohio State Buckeye traditions, stories, and swag, many people simply adopt the Buckeyes as their team. This decision often takes place within a framework of cultural factors that are often invisible and unspoken, even to the person deciding.

Congregations also make decisions within a framework governing how traditions, practices, policies, and so on are adopted and adapted. All congregations adopt and adapt to various ways of being and doing. The more inwardly focused a congregation becomes in how it adopts and adapts ideas, the more likely it is to take on swamp characteristics. The reality is just like the way someone born in Ohio may not realize all the factors in becoming a Buckeye fan. Many congregations do not realize how their process for decision making moves them toward becoming a swamp or canal.

How can congregations avoid the trap of developing a decision-making framework for adopting and adapting the wrong things? The key is to become an adept congregation.

Adept congregations are very intentional about making decisions based on missional motives rather than self-interest. Before exploring further what it means to be an adept congregation, let's consider the ways in which congregations develop a decision-making framework based upon adopting and adapting.

Adopt

The word *adopt* is important in the Bible and in our culture. Paul uses the legal language of adoption to describe the way God brings us into the fold (see Eph 1:5). We can easily relate to what Paul is saying because we are familiar with how the adoption of children occurs in our culture today. For Paul, the key is that being adopted through Jesus Christ means we take on the ways of Jesus. To adopt something is to take it on or follow in that way.

Many of us enjoy eating. At least, I do! But there comes a time when we need to cut back on our calories. We have to adopt a low-calorie diet. I did. I started to strictly follow a particular diet plan, knowing that if I stuck with the specifics of the plan, it would help me lose weight. We adopt things in our own lives all the time. The point is, we are taking something on or following something to make it our own. We are making an intentional decision to take something on and to follow it, believing it will be beneficial.

Congregations are constantly adopting things from the Christian tradition, denominational traditions, and cultural traditions. For example, Communion and baptism are part of the Christian tradition. The way a congregation decides to practice these traditions can differ depending on the congregation.

21

The Episcopal *Book of Common Prayer* is specific to a denominational tradition. Episcopal congregations still may differ on how they adopt using it. The use of screens in worship is a more recent cultural adoption by many congregations. All congregations make decisions to adopt ways of being or doing—in worship, ministry, and other areas of congregational life. These decisions are believed to be beneficial for the congregation. The decisions have ramifications for how a congregation shapes its missional identity.

The decisions we make in shaping our missional identity can be good or not so good, depending on the way a practice is adopted. For example, in 2 Kings 2:1-15, the prophet Elisha adopts the spirit of Elijah. He takes up Elijah's mantle and claims it as his own. I believe what Paul has in mind for followers of Jesus is that we should take up Jesus's mantle and claim it as our own. We become a child of God through adoption and are expected to exemplify loving God and neighbor like Jesus did.

But there are also biblical examples of adoption done poorly. In Exodus 32:1-7, the Israelites are waiting for Moses to return and they become antsy. They start complaining to Aaron that new gods need to be made. Aaron tells them to take off their gold earrings and to give them to him. (I am struck by what they are willing to give up when they think it will benefit them.) The Israelites do as Aaron asks, and he makes them a golden calf. It is not hard to guess that God is displeased with how the Israelites adopt the ways of their neighbors who worship multiple gods. This is not the sort of adoption that God intended for the Israelites. What the Israelites perceive as beneficial is not supported by a good decision-making framework.

22

Congregations face a similar decision-making dilemma as the Israelites. Consider a congregation that is in a community with a lot of children. The congregation decides to adopt a policy that only church members can use the playground. The trustees put up signs sharing the new policy. It is posted to the church webpage. What is interesting is the congregation also wants to invite new families to church. The congregation has adopted a policy to keep children away while simultaneously seeking to connect with new families. This is an extreme example, but I hope the point is clear. We make decisions to adopt things in our congregations all the time that can have negative ramifications. The perception inside the church is the policy makes sense because it protects the playground. The likely perception of those in the neighborhood is different because it says, "We do not really want your children here." We need to be mindful of what we adopt.

When we make decisions to adopt bad or inappropriate ways of being and doing, it typically leads to an inward focus. The Israelites in Exodus 32:1-7 were inwardly focused and it led them to adopt the ways of other nations. It is important that what we adopt moves us toward taking on the mantle of Jesus. What we adopt should move us toward participating in God's transforming work. It should not be something solely for our own benefit. We need to ask, "Are we benefitting ourselves, or are we seeking to touch the lives of others?" In the example of adopting a policy of barring neighborhood children from the playground, the church is frustrating the aim of touching the lives of others.

For many congregations today, the way they adopt things moves them more toward swamp rather than canal characteristics. Swamp congregations believe the decisions they are making are beneficial, but they fail to ask, "beneficial to whom?" These congregations are losing sight of what it means to be missional. They are focused on self-preservation. Rereading the story of Elisha can be helpful in this case. Elisha picks up the mantle of Elijah not so that he can have power and be revered but for the sake of continuing the work of transformation. We are called to think about adoption in this same vein.

A church's everyday decisions on what and how to adopt policies, ideas, and so on form the identity of that congregation. This formation is typically mixed, being both good and bad in most congregations. Unfortunately, too many congregations are adopting in a manner that reinforces swamp-like characteristics and not the characteristics of a reservoir or canal. Becoming more nimble in making decisions about adopting new ideas and practices is a central characteristic of adept congregations.

Adapt

After I *adopted* a set diet plan, I eventually *adapted* it to allow different food choices with the same daily calorie count. I kept the original intent, but adapted it to fit a new paradigm. The key is maintaining the same daily calorie count while making some different menu choices. We adapt various things daily to fit what we are trying to accomplish.

In Matthew 26, Jesus adapts the tradition of Passover for his disciples. Jesus tells his disciples to prepare for the Passover, the celebration of the freedom of the Israelites from slavery in Egypt (Matt 26:18). But Jesus begins to adapt the traditional celebration and redefines liberation more broadly as God forgiving us from our sins (Matt 26:26). Jesus inaugurates a new covenant to celebrate this liberation with his disciples. Jesus takes an adopted tradition and adapts it in a way that honors its original intent.

When we adapt something, the goal usually is to move us forward in a way not anticipated. Jesus helps the disciples to think differently about God's act of liberation. Adapting is making a decision to take something and shape it in a different manner that does not lose sight of the original intent. The challenge is knowing what to adapt and how to do it well.

Congregations go about adapting or modifying something to fit a new paradigm all the time.[1] For example, a congregation goes to a workshop and hears a wonderful presentation on a coffee shop ministry with millennials. The congregation could not adopt the millennial coffee house plan within its context because it is surrounded by retirement homes. Instead, the congregation adapted the idea to an afternoon tea ministry working with senior adults. This is an example of an adaptation that is done well that does not lose sight of the original intent.

There are poorly done adaptations just as there are poorly done adoptions. In many cases, a poorly done adaptation results from being inwardly focused. The adaptation does not move the church toward connecting with others but rather reinforces an insider mentality.

Paul gives us a wonderful example in 1 Corinthians 11. Some people come early and eat the Lord's Supper before others arrive. Paul admonishes those eating early for enjoying their own "private dinners" while others go hungry (1 Cor 11:20). They were focusing not on the well-being of the community but on their own well-being. What is especially upsetting to Paul is that these few do not seem to care that others have nothing to eat. Their adaptation of the Lord's Supper was done poorly.

Think about a congregation that starts a rummage sale to supplement the mission budget and outreach of the congregation. It adapts the idea from a congregation that did a community bake sale to supplement missions. The congregation will sell things at a huge discount with the goal of benefiting those who cannot afford regular retail store prices. The proceeds from the sale will go into the mission budget line. The congregation prepares for the rummage sale by collecting all kinds of items from parishioners and friends of parishioners. The day of the sale, they put a sign in the church yard to announce the sale. Parishioners and the friends of parishioners all come to support the sale.

The way in which the congregation adapts the bake sale idea is inwardly focused. The rummage sale, while supporting missions, never includes the community. The sale focuses on those in the congregation and their friends. If the goal is to benefit the community, then the congregation is somewhat off track. Certainly, putting the proceeds toward mission may ultimately benefit the community, but the rummage sale itself did not. The community was not involved in planning or even promoting the rummage sale. The adaptation of the bake sale mirrored the few individuals in the Corinth community focusing on themselves and not the well-being of the whole.

The way in which we make decisions to adapt traditions and practices should make a difference in the lives of others beyond our internal community. When we make decisions focused on our own comfort, we start down a path leading away from being missional. The way in which we adapt has significant ramifications for the congregation. Congregations that are relational and truly seeking to live out canal characteristics tend to do better at adapting in ways that are outwardly focused.

The congregation adapting the bake sale could have partnered with a community organization for the rummage sale. It could have promoted it in local businesses and shared how the proceeds will be reinvested in the community. The congregation could have adapted the bake sale in any number of ways to make it more relational and touch the lives of others. While the intent of the adaptation was good, the decision-making process along the way was not.

The decision-making process congregations rely on to adopt or adapt ideas can play out in both good and bad ways. The challenge is that too many congregations adopt and adapt in a manner that moves toward swamp characteristics and not canal characteristics. The question becomes, "What is different about those congregations who adopt and adapt in a more relational way?" This leads us to consider what it means to be an adept congregation.

Adept

In Luke 13, Jesus heals a woman who is crippled (vv. 10-17). A synagogue leader is upset with Jesus because this occurs on the Sabbath. The synagogue leader does not address Jesus with his response but the crowd. Now, right there is a lesson about how we do not address our concerns to the right person. But for our purposes, Jesus's response to the synagogue leaders is most important. Jesus adeptly reimagines the interpretation of holiness. Jesus responds in a way that bridges the legalistic interpretation of the law with the hope of being made whole. Jesus is adept at doing this sort of bridge work.

Being adept requires the ability to navigate with a high level of precision. I have watched many jets land on aircraft carriers. I am always amazed by how adept or precise a pilot must be to land the jet. It is not just the pilot's accomplishment. A team makes sure the jet lands safely. The team must navigate wind, speed, and so on to ensure a safe landing. If this is not done with a high level of precision, the consequences can be dire. The aircraft carrier team must be this adept every single day. Getting it right just some of the time is not an option.

Congregations must learn how to be adept in their decision making. The decisions they make to adopt and adapt should be done in a way that touch the lives of others. This is what Jesus does in Luke 13. Jesus is adept in how he reimagines holiness in a way that touches the lives of the woman he heals and those in the crowd.

The commandment to keep the Sabbath holy establishes six days to work and do the work that needs to be done (Exod 20:8-11). This commandment is connected to the creation account of God making the world in six days and resting on the seventh. It would be strange for Jesus to arbitrarily alter this commandment. What Jesus does is adeptly redefine the meaning of holiness for the synagogue leaders and the crowd. Holiness is not simply a matter of not doing something. It is about bringing someone more fully into community. Jesus maintains holiness by allowing a daughter of Abraham to escape the stigma of exclusion. Jesus asks, "Is this not the intent of keeping the Sabbath holy?"

We are called to be adept in the same way that Jesus navigates keeping the Sabbath holy. Jesus navigates between simply adopting the commandment in the way the synagogue leaders hoped and adapting it in a meaningless manner. The commandment is still crucial, but it is reimagined in a way that restores community. Jesus illustrates a decision-making framework that moves us toward missional engagement.

Imagine a scenario in which a congregation has to deal with the very challenging issue of the son of a parishioner returning to the congregation after being in prison for robbery. One way of dealing with the situation is to avoid the elephant in the room. No one says anything. This is often how congregations will respond to such a challenging issue. Another way is for individuals to whisper behind the family's back, making comments like, "I can't believe they are bringing Charlie back to church. You know he spent time in prison." The truth is, most folks sense when you are talking about them.

An adept way of dealing with this situation is for the pastor or other church leaders to meet with the family and welcome Charlie home. They name the elephant in the room by acknowledging that some people will be uncomfortable with Charlie's return. But they also affirm the commitment to make the church a hospitable space. The leadership begins this process by asking the family, "What is helpful?" The goal is not to scare the family away or make the congregation out to be bad people. The goal is to navigate the reality of the challenge ahead and the unique possibility for something new and wonderful. Making space for the new and wonderful is what moves Christians toward the new heaven. One never knows where a new opportunity may lead. In this situation, if the congregation is truly adept, it can become a place where other returning citizens can experience God.

Being adept requires making decisions that will expand our reach and allow us to touch more lives. This does not happen overnight or without intention. Four practices can help us be a more adept congregation. This is not an exhaustive list, but one that helps a congregation to get on the right track.

1. Discernment

The word *discern* is used all the time. One is hard-pressed to read or hear a presentation related to Christianity without some reference to discernment. What is discernment? How do you do it? Outside church culture, it usually refers to exercising sound judgment. Within church culture, discernment takes on a spiritual dimension. It involves having a special knowledge coming from God to aid in the decision process. While sound judgment is still integral to how discernment happens within church culture, that judgment is based in God leading the process and not our own insight. For instance, congregations will often talk about discerning a path forward to be more vital. The congregation is saying it is counting on God to lead them in judging the next steps to take. At least that is what the congregation should be saying.

But then the question becomes, "How do we do this?" If it were as easy as saying, "We will now discern how to move forward," then everyone would do it and the goal of vitality would be quickly achieved. Unfortunately, discernment is not easy. We have to listen for God. It requires patience and an openness to hearing from God. God may speak to us through scripture, through music, through other individuals, or by some

30

other sign. We must remain prayerful and pay attention. In one congregation, five unrelated people came to the pastor in a three-month period to say the community really needed a summer camp for children and asked if the church could help. God was speaking through those individuals and the pastor listened. Discernment requires that we be open to the various ways God helps us make important judgments.

Let me be clear. The exercise of discernment is not only for pastors. All Christians are called to discern God's direction. A congregation discerning a major decision should not sit and wait on the pastor. The whole congregation should be in discernment together. One of the ways that we know something is truly of God is when many different people start hearing the same thing or receiving the same affirmation.

Adept congregations are characterized by ongoing discernment of what God is saying. Decisions on what to adopt or adapt are based not on our human judgment but by following God's lead. Jesus often prays to God before going forward. We should follow in Jesus's footsteps and do the same. Good decisions start with being in touch with God.

2. Connecting to Mission and Community

An adept congregation decides the way it adopts and adapts based on its overarching mission. While most churches have a mission statement, many do not use it in decision making. A good mission statement should help a congregation get where it is trying to go. A good mission statement will often have key words like *connecting*, *serving*, and *growing*—action words that require the congregation to do something.

31

It is harder for congregations to get where they want to go if they make decisions that ignore their mission statement. A congregation whose mission statement centers around serving others but decides to start a Saturday fellowship ministry for congregants is ignoring its mission. There is nothing wrong with a Saturday fellowship, but it is not in line with the mission of that congregation. Adept congregations make decisions in light of their mission. This requires having a good mission statement because a poor one will still leave a congregation scrambling.

The adept congregation connects not only to its mission but also to the broader community. Decisions are made with the community in mind. Instead of a Saturday fellowship that focuses on parishioners visiting each other, the congregation hosts neighborhood gatherings where all are welcome and relationships can be built with new individuals. By shifting the focus of the Saturday fellowship, it can touch the lives of those in the community.

Adept congregations take their mission statement seriously and are continuously looking for ways to engage the community. This means the decisions to adopt or adapt ways of being and doing have to fit the mission and engage the community. What a difference it would make if congregations made decisions in this way! Deciding whether to start a new ministry is easier because there are certain clear criteria. Always asking if a new idea embodies the mission and engages the community will help to prevent a congregation from making bad decisions.

3. Evaluation

Adept congregations have processes in place to evaluate decisions and programs. In some congregations, worn-out traditions linger on because no one takes the time to evaluate them. For example, one congregation started having a children's choir at the Christmas Eve service at a time when many children were present in the life of the church. Ten years later, they retain this tradition, even though there are only a few children and those who started the ministry are now in high school. The tradition of the children's choir just continues in perpetuity because the congregation never re-evaluated the program.

Congregations should evaluate decisions like maintaining the children's choir annually. Is the choir still fulfilling our mission? Is the choir still touching the lives of those beyond the congregation? Annual evaluation allows a congregation to keep the program, pivot, or decide something has run its course. The congregation with the depleted children's choir could pivot and decide the time is right for a teen choir. Another alternative would be simply to say the children's choir has run its course and end it, at least for the time being. This does not preclude restarting the ministry when there are more children. It is important to evaluate continually and then act based on the evaluation.

The initial criteria for evaluation should include the congregation's mission statement and the goal of touching lives in the community. As you get in the habit of doing evaluations, you may develop different criteria, but avoiding evaluation altogether is not an option. While the church is not a business, churches can learn from successful businesses the importance of evaluating what is working and what is not working. If a church has two choirs and the church is full every time Choir A sings but mostly empty for Choir B, it's time to evaluate why.

It does not mean Choir B no longer sings, but the data cannot be ignored.

Adept congregations evaluate because they seek to remain active participants with God in the transformation of lives. Adept congregations are not beholden to sustaining a pet ministry just because it was started by a founding member. The founding member started it because it was suitable for that time. The key is to figure out what is suitable for today. A good evaluation process is necessary for this determination.

4. Forming Good Habits

Adept congregations don't leave things to chance or happenstance. They make sound decision making a matter of habit. Too often congregations will try something new, and things will change for a short period of time, but soon the congregation slips back into the old ways of doing something. When a congregation is intentional in establishing new habits, changes are more likely to stick. A new habit that becomes second nature within a church is more likely to have a lasting impact.

Growing up, I had a friend who would dribble a basketball, switching hands, while walking to school. He did this every day the weather permitted. By the time he went out for the varsity squad, handling a basketball had become second nature to him. He could dribble with either hand, never thinking about the mechanics of the action.

For a congregation to institute a new habit, it needs to be practiced over and over again, like the dribbling of the basketball. Start with just one or two key decisions and work to routinize the process until it becomes habitual. Then expand your focus as the congregation gets better at the process. Starting small allows for trial and error as you move the congregation toward a new way of being and doing. Making good decisions habitually will move the congregation in the right direction.

An adept congregation discerns, connects, evaluates, and makes good decision making a matter of habit. It doesn't take much imagination to figure out why swamp congregations are not adept. Swamp congregations typically are not very discerning. They tend to rely on their own instincts, even when those instincts are not proving fruitful. Swamp congregations rarely connect decisions to the mission statement and are unconcerned about engaging the community. There is no evaluation process in place and things continue to happen in just the same way simply because it has always been that way. Their habits lead to poor decision making, not good decision making.

A reservoir congregation is somewhat better. In reservoir congregations, some individuals are committed to discernment, but it is usually not a community-wide effort. They make connections to engage the community, but these connections usually do not align with the mission statement. And the evaluation process is hit or miss, depending on the leader in charge of particular areas of ministry. These congregations have a mix of good and bad decision-making habits.

Canal congregations are the most adept. I say *most adept* because all congregations have room for growth. Canal congregations embed discernment into the decision-making process. They are intentional about connecting to the mission statement and engaging the community. Evaluation is a critical component for all areas of ministry, and the congregation is not afraid to pivot. Most importantly, canal congregations work hard to develop good decision-making habits.

Adept congregations thrive because they are better at making decisions than most congregations. The reality is, most congregations are a work in progress. As you seek to make your congregation more adept, don't try to do everything at once. You might start with decisions related to your church building and then continue to expand as you become more proficient. Is the congregation discerning in terms of the use of the building? Does the use of the building fulfill the mission? Is the building a tool for engaging the community? Is there a process in place to evaluate building use decisions? And how can that process become habitual?

Between a Rock and Hard Place

An adept congregation develops a decision-making framework that effectively adopts and adapts ways of being and doing. This framework sets the stage for a strong missional existence. For a struggling congregation, the challenge of becoming adept may seem like a pipe dream. Struggling churches may not even be aware of how their decision making is governed mostly by self-interest. It may be difficult to figure out how to capitalize on the good things while not allowing poor decisions to become habitual. A struggling congregation can literally be a few poor decisions away from becoming a swamp. Congregations that are doing well struggle to figure out how to keep it going—how to keep in place a framework to thrive missionally. Virtually every congregation feels caught between moving forward and falling back. A rock and a hard place.

Here are a few discussion questions to help your congregation become more adept:

What traditions, policies, and so on have you *adopted* in the last year?

What traditions, policies, and so on have you *adapted* in the last year?

What were your criteria for adopting and adapting these traditions or policies?

Is there one ministry area where you can begin using the decision-making framework of an adept congregation?

Answering these questions will begin a process to help your church become an adept congregation. Even within already adept congregations, these questions can be helpful in certain ministries or areas that are not functioning as well as they could.

Adept congregation are in a position to influence others toward living missionally. The next chapter explores the importance of influence.

ESTHER INTERLUDE TWO

Then Esther sent this reply to Mordecai: "Go, gather together all the Jews who are in Susa, and fast for me. Do not eat or drink for three days, night or day. I and my attendants will fast as you do. When this is done, I will go to the king, even though it is against the law. And if I perish, I perish."
So Mordecai went away and carried out all of Esther's instructions.

—Esther 4:15-19

In Esther 4 and 5, we see how Esther is called upon to play various leadership roles to move the community forward. Esther understands her role as a part of the royal court. She has been given a privileged position, but one that requires her to follow protocol. In chapter 4, Esther is both follower and leader. At first, Mordecai is still in charge and directing Esther. But she comes to understand that she has to play a more influential role. By verse 15, the roles reverse, and Esther instructs Mordecai to lead the community in a three-day fast. By the end of the chapter, she has taken on a more challenging and risky leadership role of an astute advisor to the king. She is able to influence him in a generative (productive) way, transforming the destiny of her community.

We all play various leadership roles in our communities, depending on the circumstances.

Think about your church community and the different roles necessary for it to move forward. Do not think about positions or titles, but the actual functions and tasks needed to move the community forward. The title of pastor signals a certain level of authority, but not necessarily influence. The title of trustee chair gives one a level of authority, but not necessarily influence. Whatever role you play, it is important to figure out where you have generative influence.

A pastor decides she wants to change the format of worship. She knows this will be a big change. So, she starts having coffee conversations with all the players involved in worship. She invites all of them to a one-day workshop on worship led by a trusted consultant. The pastor has another round of one-on-one conversations to hear input from the team. Six months later, the pastor introduces the new worship format. Because she used her influence in a generative manner to set the stage, most of the team is excited about the change.

We can spin the same narrative in the opposite direction. In this case, the pastor walks into the worship meeting and announces, "This is our new format." A few people on the team see the advantages but would have liked some time to think about what it means for their roles. Most of the people are upset because they feel they had no say in the matter. This is using influence in a negative manner.

What lessons can we learn from Esther? She realizes the risk she is taking in assuming this responsibility. She uses her influence to set the stage. She does not immediately ask the king to save her people. First, she asks the king to come to a banquet with Haman. It is important to note that Esther could have been distracted from her goal when the king twice says to her, "What is your request? Even up to half the kingdom, it will be given to you" (Esth 5:3, 6). What a powerful temptation to forget her goal! Twice, the king offers her as much as half his kingdom, but she does not allow herself to be distracted from what she hopes to accomplish for her community.

We must not only set the stage for change by using generative influence, we need to avoid distraction. In the scenario above, the pastor seeking to change the worship format sought input from those on her team who had to deal with this new challenge. In one meeting, a member offered to pay all the expenses to bring in one of the top vocalists in the area. The pastor understood this would generate excitement, but it was not the direction in which she hoped to move the community. This change would distract from her ultimate objective.

We learn from Esther that we all play various roles in the community at different times. The real key to our effectiveness in these roles is not title or position, but influence. We also learn we have to be careful when we set out to move the community to a new place because distractions will eventually come our way.

The focus in the next chapter shifts from thinking about the type of communities where we live out our faith to the importance of influence in helping a community to move forward. Helping a community change is never easy, and position or title are not enough to move congregations toward living missionally.

INFLUENCE

There is often a difference between who is in charge and who has influence. The person in charge may have authority by virtue of title or position. The person with influence may have it by virtue of wisdom, expertise, age, financial support of the institution, and so on. The way we gain influence is different from the way we come into a position. This is one reason why it is generally hard for a son or daughter to succeed a parent in ministry. The parent not only had the position but had influence gained through years in ministry. The son or daughter may assume the title and position but generally does not come into the role with the same degree of influence.

Title and position may allow you to make decisions and give commands. But influence is required to move a community in a different direction. How do you gain influence if you do not have it in the beginning? How do you keep influence if you need to make major changes? Gaining and keeping influence is not a product of leadership style but develops from the way a leader cultivates generative influence. This equips them to help the community to make generative decisions that move the community forward.

There is a connection between the ability of leaders to use their influence in helpful ways and the missional vitality of the congregation. Thriving congregations tend to have leaders who have generative influence, and this spills out into the greater community. These leaders find productive ways to move things forward. In swamp congregations, leaders tend to exert non-productive influence and spend more time on in-fighting. Most congregations are somewhere in the middle.

Eight factors contribute to generative influence. Leadership in congregations that are struggling typically only exhibit a few of these factors. Those in thriving congregations tend to exhibit more of these factors.

1. Relationships

It should be no surprise that the influence of leaders flows from their relationships with others. Generally, we listen to those who have built strong relationships with us. They have earned the right to share challenging ideas or information with us. They have earned the right to seek our support. Someone who is not relational may still have other types of influence. But building and maintaining relationships with others helps a leader develop generative influence.

Moses understood this when God asked him to free the Israelites from Egyptian bondage. Moses realized he did not have relational clout with the Israelites, but Aaron and Miriam did. Had Moses moved ahead without assistance from Aaron and Miriam, he would not have had the necessary influence because he lacked relational connections.

Leaders need to be astute in developing relational clout, taking the time to meet and talk with others and learning to rely on people who can enhance their clout by vouching for them. A leader can have the best ideas in the world, but without relational credibility, it is difficult to get a hearing. Intentionally developing relational clout gives a leader the platform to have challenging and productive conversations. Otherwise, even the best ideas would fall on deaf ears. When a leader relies only on a title to garner influence, it limits the impact of their leadership. Several other factors are important in developing relational clout, such as strengthening relationships with people who have their own influence. But the importance of relational clout in moving a community forward should not be underestimated.

2. Knowledge

It is important to have a certain level of competence in areas in which you seek influence. You don't need to know everything, but people need to believe you know something about the subject at hand. Imagine your daughter coming home and saying her new math teacher does not know math. He has only taught history, which is the primary area of his expertise. As a parent, you would be concerned if a math teacher has no knowledge of math, no matter how smart he may be. You would want your child to be taught by someone with expertise in math.

To be influential in leading people toward something new and different, a leader needs some base of knowledge. A leader who knows the lay of the land has a better chance of success. This means doing your homework before presenting an idea to the community. It may sound like a great idea for your congregation to start a day care center. But do you know anything about what it takes to start a day care center? What types of permits or licenses are needed? What is the appropriate price to charge? The idea may be a good one, but others won't buy into it unless you demonstrate the appropriate knowledge.

Most individuals look to leaders to share insights that will help the community make good choices. Even if you don't have firsthand knowledge, you can do the necessary research. A part of being knowledgeable is knowing where to go for more information. Knowledge isn't the only factor that goes into good decision making. But when seeking to move others in a new direction, it is important to share insights that demonstrate a high degree of competency.

3. Trust

Trust is closely related to relational influence. But having a strong relationship with someone doesn't mean we would trust that person to take on a particular role. I may think Perry is a wonderful individual. I really enjoy my conversations with Perry. But this does not mean I automatically trust him to be the treasurer of the congregation. While I have no problem relating to Perry, I do not trust that he is the right person for this particular role.

It is also important that people trust the leader's vision. The two are not always connected. I may trust Beth but not her vision. If I am not convinced that Beth's idea to add a day care center to the church is the right way to go, all the influence in the world will not change my perspective. I do not trust the vision.

As leaders, we need to help others trust our ability to perform in a role or to complete a task. And we need to help them trust the vision we journey toward. We help others trust our ability when they experience us as competent. This may take time, especially if we are new. We have a greater opportunity of influencing others when they trust our ability to do the job. If they believe we can do the job, then we can influence the way in which they live into the vision.

It is sometimes the case that a leader is highly competent in a leadership role but is still not considered trustworthy. This is often the case in small church communities when a new leader is viewed as an outsider. The pastor coming in from the outside may be extremely competent, but those within the community will not automatically trust any outsider. In these situations, trust often develops when the new pastor works with the community to achieve a common goal. The pastor cannot change the fact that he or she is an outsider. But working together with the community to reach a mutual goal is a key step to build trust.

4. Honesty

To influence others, it is important to be honest. When people can believe what a leader tells them, they are more likely to journey with that leader. As leaders, we must be open about what we know and don't know, about what we can and cannot do. We can admit where we need help and when we have made a mistake because no one is capable of being perfect and doing everything perfectly all the time. Instead of trying to cover up our mistakes and limitations, it is better to be candid about them.

In the Gospel of Mark, Jesus heals a boy who had suffered seizures for years. Jesus tells the boy's father, "All things can be done for the one who believes." The father first responds, "I believe." Then he becomes brutally honest and says, "Help my unbelief" (Mark 9:23-24 NRSV). The father realizes that being honest about his doubt is not a liability. Leaders who remain confident while being honest about their shortcomings will be more influential. Admitting your shortcomings goes a long way in proving you have the authenticity and integrity needed to build relationships and trust. People are willing to journey with those who have integrity.

Sometimes even our best ideas don't work out as we hoped. Honestly admitting when something hasn't worked out as planned helps establish our credibility. It signals to others that we are not captive to our fragile ego. Admitting that an idea hasn't worked out as planned should not be perceived as failure. It demonstrates an ability to assess outcomes objectively and change course when needed. This type of honest assessment is about making the best decisions to move forward toward God's calling.

5. Investing in Others

To gain influence, leaders have to invest in others, committing time and effort to know and encourage them. People need to believe a leader is interested in who they are and what they do. Jesus was committed to investing in others. He invested in Mary, Martha, Peter, and others. Jesus was on a mission. But he did not pursue his mission at the expense of caring about the needs and dreams of others. Jesus took the time to eat, converse, and journey with others. Our investment in others cannot be a superficial endeavor. We must truly invest in the well-being of individuals we are entrusted to lead.

When we take the time to really listen to others, they are more willing to listen to us. If a church trustee is tasked with updating the youth room, that trustee should take the time to see how the youth use the room and listen to their ideas. It may be tempting to skip engaging the youth to move the project forward quickly. But once the project is complete, and the trustee is organizing a churchwide cleanup day, the trustee will have more influence in persuading the youth to participate if the trustee invested time engaging the youth in deciding how to update the youth room.

It is hard for a leader who is completely detached from the community to have influence. While it is important to set appropriate boundaries, an influential leader takes time to discover the hopes and dreams of others and help them achieve their dreams. When we make this type of investment in others, we will find that they are more willing to invest in us. Leaders cannot simply expect others to give and do if they do not reciprocate by investing in them.

6. A Clear Direction

Mapping out a clear direction is critical to establishing influence. If I am planning to drive from Baltimore, Maryland, to San Francisco, California, I need to map out the preferred route for the journey. I could just head west. But if I want to visit family in Alabama on the way, I need to head south before heading west. If I want to see friends in New York, I need to go north before going west. The point is, mapping out the direction is essential to getting where we want to go in an efficient manner.

An urban congregation studied census data to determine trends in their surrounding community. The study confirmed the community was gentrifying at a rapid pace and the neighborhood would look completely different within about seven years. Some church members assumed this meant the church needed to relocate to a different location where the demographics of the surrounding community would be more like those of the congregation. Others believed the church should stay put and try and reach those in the gentrifying neighborhood. The congregation never settled on a clear direction. And without a clear direction, no action was taken and the influence of the leaders was compromised.

There may never be 100 percent agreement within a congregation about the best way forward. Yet, an influential leader seeks a consensus on where the church should be headed and how it should get there. The congregation described above divided over whether to relocate or stay in the same community. It needed to have some challenging conversations related to their mission and vision. Regardless of the direction chosen, certain individuals may leave the church. But avoiding the elephant in the room only leads to further decline. We are better able to influence others when the direction we are headed in is clear.

7. Flexibility

Flexibility is another key factor contributing to a leader's influence. Being flexible doesn't mean being wishy-washy or indecisive. A wishy-washy leader blows with the wind. One person comes to them and makes the case for letting kids have food and drinks in the Sunday school classrooms and the leader agrees. The next person comes to them and makes the case for putting a stop to kids having food and drinks in the classroom and the leader changes their mind.

Instead of just agreeing with the last person in the room, a flexible leader takes time to dig more deeply into the issue and learn the underlying cause of the problem in hopes of finding a compromise. For example, the leader might offer a compromise allowing food and drinks in the Sunday school classrooms on the third Sunday of the month when the room is used for children's church, with the understanding that those hosting the activities will also take responsibility for cleanup. This solution recognizes that the "no food or drinks in the classroom" policy served the purpose of keeping the classrooms clean. But it also acknowledged the needs of hungry and thirsty children.

Being flexible is tricky because some individuals will try to take advantage of you. But if you never show flexibility, you may be perceived as rigid and uncompromising. Learning to be flexible in the right way builds a leader's influence. When others see a leader's willingness to compromise, they are more willing to do the same. Great leaders are typically decisive but understand the importance of being flexible to help move people forward missionally.

8. Inspiration

Influential leaders inspire others. Being inspirational is not about having a charismatic personality. It's about motivating others to work hard and reach higher levels of spiritual maturity. Before going back to school for my master of divinity degree, I worked in the benefits industry. One of the most successful managers was introverted and quiet. But he was great at helping others feel their work made a significant contribution to the company. And this inspired other employees to excel.

Congregations tend to excel when individual members are inspired to use their gifts to fulfill the church's mission. It is easier to be inspiring when things are going well. It's more challenging to be inspiring when the going gets tough. But in a struggling church, the secret is to celebrate even the smallest success in order to inspire people toward greater success. For example, vacation Bible school this year had five more participants from the neighborhood than last year. Celebrating a small success can be a building block toward other successes—five more children in vacation Bible school might lead to a more successful back-to-school program in September.

Influential leaders find ways to inspire others to excel. Inspiring the community is not the job of one person. It is something all leaders must do if the community is to thrive.

These eight factors are not new. But it is helpful to understand their importance in establishing a leader's influence so that a community can participate more fully in God's mission. The goal of all leaders, regardless of their leadership role or leadership style, should be to influence others to participate in God's mission.

No one person is likely to have all eight characteristics. But a good team will collectively embody these different characteristics. If I am an introvert who likes thinking and working alone, I might make sure there are others on my team who are more relational. It does not mean I'm excused from building relationships, but it allows different team members to play to their strengths.

Adept congregations make good decisions. Leaders facilitate generative decision making by using their influence to get others to buy into decisions that will move the congregation forward. Leaders who influence others in non-generative ways tend to struggle. And their congregations are more likely to resemble a swamp than a canal.

Generative Influence

Adept congregations make decisions that put the congregation in a position to thrive. The role of leaders is to help influence the community to make generative decisions. Generative decisions move the community forward. They transform individual lives and the life of the broader community. In other words, a generative decision moves a congregation toward becoming a canal church.

How can leaders use their influence this way? Think about a congregation considering a building project. A generative dialogue would address not only the needs of the congregation, but it would also anticipate how a building project could impact the community. How might the project lead to new partnerships between the congregation and broader community? How might it help build relationships? Will it help the congregation invest in others? Leaders seeking to influence the congregation toward a generative decision see the building project as a part of the congregation's overall mission and not something that just benefits insiders.

What about the church experiencing declining attendance? Too often, churches seeking to reach new people assume that all they need to do is introduce new people to the church. Once these newcomers realize how wonderful the church is, they will want to join. A leader seeking to influence a congregation with this mindset toward a generative decision must first help the congregation be more honest in assessing the reality of its situation. If the neighborhood is attracting young families whose children play soccer on Sundays, it is probably a losing proposition to invite them to Sunday morning events. If there are more Spanish-speaking immigrants coming into the neighborhood and no one in the congregation speaks Spanish, just asking them to come to worship won't work. Adept leaders help congregations see their situation objectively.

Next, a leader needs to help the congregation decide how to reach new people and what they will invest to reach them. The congregation may decide it is willing to invest time and resources to offer weekday worship or Bible study for soccer families who can't come on Sundays. The key is asking if this investment makes sense and if it can be sustained. If no one is willing to give time during the week to support the new outreach ministry, this option does not make sense. Leaders have to influence the decision-making process by confirming that the investment makes sense.

Finally, leaders need to help the congregation build relationships with those it seeks to reach. The goal of reaching Spanish-speaking immigrant families is admirable, but how will the congregation build relationships with them? Maybe the congregation starts a tutoring program to help the children of immigrant families with their homework—once they determine this is an investment of time and resources that makes sense. The key is giving thought to how the congregation is going to be relational and not just assuming it will happen by magic.

In a generative approach to decision making, leaders are aware of the eight factors lending them influence. And they use those levels of influence to promote a dialogue that moves the church toward fulfilling God's calling. Generative influence moves a congregation forward in the right way because it impacts the decision-making process in the right way. While there is no one way to accomplish this goal, here are three things to keep in mind.

1. Start by asking the right questions.

Lovett Weems, distinguished professor of church leadership at Wesley Theological Seminary, recommends a maxim:

"Leaders do not need answers. Leaders must have the right questions."[1] Starting with the right questions is fundamental. Having the right answer to the wrong question does nothing to advance the ball. What are the right questions? Right questions focus on the underlying issue. Right questions address the concerns and perspectives of the broader community and not just those of insiders. Right questions require a deeper dialogue and not simple "yes" and "no" answers.

2. Have the right people at the table.

This can be tricky. Often churches will involve too many or too few people in decision making. Initially, you want key stakeholders and influencers at the table—individuals who have an interest in the discussion and can eventually help you to persuade others. If you have a good communication process, you need fewer people at the table because relevant information can be shared later with others.

3. Make sure everyone understands their roles.

Regardless of official positions, titles, or roles, everyone at the table needs to understand what part they play in the process. The roles they are called upon to play may be different than their official roles. For example, the director of Christian education has no official role in church finances. But because she has the spiritual gift of giving and has faithfully supported the congregation for years, she may take on the role of spokesperson for the stewardship campaign.

As you develop your own process for generative influence, remember these things: focus on right questions, bring the right people to the table, and make sure that each person knows his or her role in the matter at hand. These three strategies will help your congregation to become adept at the decision-making process.

Between a Rock and a Hard Place

A leader's ability to influence decisions in a generative way is critical. Without generative decision making, a congregation can end up resembling a swamp. But it's not easy. Congregations are continually having to make decisions on multiple fronts. More and more often, it's volunteer leaders who are making the tough choices. And in smaller congregations, it's often the same small group of people responsible for all of the decisions. It can be harder to influence someone with whom you have a long history!

What I know is that the current process in most congregations is not working. More and more of these congregations are moving in the direction of a swamp rather than a reservoir or canal. In most congregations, the idea of trying something different is typically met with suspicion. But continuing to do things the same way can be a fruitless endeavor.

A congregation is caught between a rock and a hard place when its only choices seem to be hitting the same wall over and over again or taking a blind leap of faith. But there is a way forward that leads to great vitality. Answering these questions may start you down the right path.

> What characteristics of generative influence are currently being lived out in your congregation?

> What characteristics are missing from your community? Who are the individuals who can supply what is missing, and how do you get them involved?

What is the current process for influencing decisions?

What is a first step your congregation can take to
    implement this process?

How are you developing the questions that will lead to
    good decisions?

Do you have a process for helping individuals understand
    the need to play different roles in the community?

ESTHER INTERLUDE THREE

Then Esther sent this reply to Mordecai: "Go, gather together all the Jews who are in Susa, and fast for me. Do not eat or drink for three days, night or day. I and my attendants will fast as you do. When this is done, I will go to the king, even though it is against the law. And if I perish, I perish."
　　　　　　　　　　　　　　　　　　　　　　　　　—Esther 5:15-16

At the beginning of chapter 4, Esther understands her mission from the perspective of an insider. But by verse 15, Esther comes to understand that her mission must include the broader community. And for the best chance of success, certain practices are required.

Many congregations never make the switch from being inwardly focused to understanding that their mission includes the broader community. The church community exists to meet the needs of its members. Think about why most people decide to join one faith community or another. Generally, they are looking for a church that can do something for them, in one way or another. Few are motivated to join a congregation based on what the congregation might need from them.

A good analogy is people's motivation to join fraternities and sororities. Fraternities and sororities do charity work and engage in other community service endeavors. But few individuals are attracted to one particular Greek organization over another based on their charity work. Getting someone involved in charity work is certainly a positive byproduct of the decision to join a Greek organization. But in my experience, most people join fraternities and sororities for networking, fellowship, and status. Getting involved in charity work is a positive outcome of the decision to join but rarely the main motivation.

Unfortunately, the same is generally true when people join churches. Rarely is a desire to support the mission of the church the main reason people connect with a congregation. People generally select a church because they like the ministries, the preaching, or the people. None of these motivations are bad. But if these are the most important reasons for people to choose a church, they are unlikely to want these things to change. It's easy to see how this leads to an insider mentality rather than a missional mindset.

Esther realizes that as much as she may want things to stay the same, it's not likely to happen. Circumstances compel her to shift from an insider mentality to one that considers the well-being of the broader community. This was no doubt a scary change for Esther, just as it can be a scary change for a congregation. But the key practice of fasting helped Esther embrace the change.

Similarly, certain key practices can help a congregation make the change from an insider mentality to a perspective that includes the broader community. The next chapter outlines characteristics of missional congregations. It will explain how congregations that include the broader community embody these practices differently than inwardly focused congregations.

It is challenging for a church to open itself to the broader community, but not impossible if we start with the practices that can shift our perspective and make us more outwardly focused.

Chapter Four

MISSIONAL CHARACTERISTICS

In the introduction to this book, I introduced the term *missional* to describe God inviting us into the ongoing work of transforming the world. This work of transformation is practical, spiritual, and directed toward something new. In chapter 2, I introduced three questions for congregations. Question 1: "Do you want to be missional?" Question 2: "Are you willing to change in order to be missional?" and Question 3: "Do you know what is required to be missional?" The focus of this chapter is on Question 2 and Question 3.

Every congregation has a different starting point for answering these questions, depending on whether they display the dominant characteristics of a swamp, reservoir, or canal. But no matter the starting point, it is key that every congregation focus on how to move forward and avoid falling backward. Adept decision making can help a congregation take a step forward, which is particularly important for swamp and reservoir congregations.

Understanding the four key characteristics of missional congregations can help a congregation that wants to move forward and live more missionally. Missional congregations are

63

incarnational, sacramental, creational, and *eschatological.* Translating these theological terms in everyday language, we can say that missional congregations are *contextual, communal, innovative,* and *visionary.* As congregations become more adept at living out these missional characteristics, they will exhibit more canal traits.

incarnational	⟶	**contextual**
sacramental	⟶	**communal**
creational	⟶	**innovative**
eschatological	⟶	**visionary**

Contextual

The opening chapter of John's Gospel is helpful in understanding what it means to be incarnational or contextual. Perhaps you are familiar with these words from the King James Bible: "The Word was made flesh and dwelt among us" (John 1:14a). Eugene Peterson's presentation of the Bible in contemporary language puts it this way: "The Word became flesh and blood, and moved into the neighborhood" (John 1:14a MSG). This image of "moving into the neighborhood" captures in everyday language the nature of the incarnation of Christ. Jesus is present and real right where we live, right before our eyes. We literally can reach out and touch Jesus. And Jesus in return can touch us.

What does it mean to be an incarnational or contextual church? An incarnational church is present and real right where we live. Those in the community can touch the church. And the church can touch them. For a church to be missional, to participate in God's transforming work, it must be contextual. It must touch others and be touched by others. How does this characteristic apply to swamp, reservoir, and canal churches?

Swamp Churches—A swamp congregation has little or no contact with the community. A swamp congregation is not becoming flesh and blood because a church that is not alive and vital cannot become flesh and blood. In fact, the swamp congregation is dying and returning to dust. A dying congregation is moving in the opposite direction of incarnation.

Picture a congregation that is surrounded by some houses, a school not too far away, and one or two small businesses. The congregation's only connections to the community are collecting money for backpacks at the start of school and assembling a Thanksgiving basket for a needy family. They have no personal contact with the school children or the needy family. The congregation cannot figure out why no one comes to worship or Bible study. In its mind, it is engaging the community. Remember, being contextual requires touching others and others touching you. This congregation is to some extent touching others, but they do not allow others to touch them.

Because swamp churches do not share themselves with others, they cannot become flesh and blood in their neighborhoods. The swamp congregation described above holds the mindset that it does its part, but people don't reciprocate. The reality is the congregation is still operating with an inward mentality; it does nothing to allow those in the community to touch and see that they are real.

Reservoir Churches—A reservoir church has contact with the community. People come to its clothing closet or monthly soup meal. It is touching those in the community and to some extent allowing those in the community to touch them. Unlike a swamp congregation, folks in the community know the reservoir church exists. When they encounter the congregation, they are made comfortable because people in the congregation are polite, but they are not made to feel welcome in a sense of being known. A reservoir church becomes flesh in the sense of becoming a familiar place that provides a service, sometimes even a necessary service. The church is a place to go for goods, but it remains only one of many places to go for goods. Those who come do not experience the fullness of being known. They are treated like clients and feel like clients, just as they would at any other social agency. They experience the physical presence of the congregation, but most of them never experience the life-giving blood that is transforming.

Canal Churches—A canal congregation becomes flesh and blood in the community, touching the lives of others and allowing others to touch it. It does so by taking an active interest in the lives of those in the community, by going to the people rather than expecting people to come to them. It builds relationships daily by meeting and engaging people away from the church edifice, not simply showing up for worship on Sunday. A canal congregation knows its neighbors and prays for them daily. A canal congregation partners with local organizations for the benefit of the community. It is part of the lifeblood of the community and the community would not be the same without it. A canal congregation is contextual because it is committed to being part of the daily lives of those around the church. This must be a congregation-wide effort, not just something the pastor does. Each person in the church can be a channel running between church and community. This is how a canal congregation is fully present and real in a community.

Communal

We use the word *community* in relation to many different entities in society and the church. Most of us participate in several different communities at the same time. We may be part of a work community, a community where we live, some other organization like a sorority or fraternity, and so on. Each of these different types of communities is bound together by a common story, a shared narrative that shapes the ways members of the community engage one another. For example, a work community's story may recall the company's founding and the colorful characters that have made an impact over the years. The story may also feature the traditions and practices that bind people together. Such a story may be inviting to new people, or it may deter others from feeling they are part of that company's community.

The church is no different. It also has a story with colorful characters. It has traditions and practices that bond individuals together. For many Christians, baptism and Communion are the central elements of those traditions and practices. Baptism and Communion recall the broader Christian story, but they also capture the story of the local congregation. The importance of baptism and Communion to the Christian community cannot be understated. Through baptism one becomes part of the great cloud of witnesses across Christian traditions, but also part of a specific local congregation. Partaking of Communion, one continues to live out the connection between God and neighbor.

In both baptism and Communion, the community shares its common story and continues to participate in that story. In baptism, we enter a community that commits to form us as we grow in discipleship. In Communion, we live out our discipleship by sharing God's grace as it has been shared with us. Although baptism is a one-time event, the work of formation is ongoing. Communion—whether we partake weekly, monthly, or according to some other schedule—gives us an opportunity to be God's ambassadors. At the Lord's Table, we are renewed for that work. Communion nourishes us for our work as disciples. That includes accepting our individual and communal calling to be God's ambassadors in the community. We truly must give ourselves away as Jesus gave himself away for us.

Swamp Churches—Swamp congregations may like the traditions of baptism and Communion but never truly embody the story they tell. The truth is, most swamp congregations have very few baptisms because there is little new life in these churches. They may come to the Communion Table monthly, just because they are in the habit of doing so, but they do not recognize how this sacrament links them to a story larger than themselves. In swamp congregations, the story is flat because participants are just going through the motions. They take the consecrated elements but are unmoved by the spiritual encounter. A swamp congregation is more interested in preserving the tradition of what has happened in the past and misses the ongoing call to live the story in the present and future.

A community that no longer sees itself as living the story is going to die. It begins to develop a story of hoarding and focusing on itself. Their story only takes place within the church walls. It does not extend to those outside who may hunger for a new story.

A living story comes to life through action. If you have ever watched a movie through 3D glasses, it appears that the action is jumping off the screen and coming right at you. The story feels alive. Maintaining a tradition is not a bad thing. But if it becomes rote, it does not bring the story to life, just like the story never comes alive in a bad movie where the actors are obviously just mailing in their performances. A congregation is called to live the story and not simply mail it in.

Reservoir Churches—A reservoir congregation is living out the story. Some people in the congregation may do things by rote, but most people see themselves as participants in the story. These congregations have more baptisms than swamp congregations. And in some cases, they start forming individuals in the story at a young age. These congregations are taking the story of Communion seriously and giving themselves away in some fashion.

The challenge for these congregations is the tendency to do *for* people instead of *with* people. Imagine a congregation trying to reach a group of college students. The congregation forms a committee to determine how to reach the students. They decide the best approach is a Saturday event of some type around lunchtime. They are all very excited and start making extravagant plans to welcome the students to the Saturday event. They ask the few students who are in the congregation to help them spread the word. These students agree to spread the word but share that Saturday at noon is not a good time because of football and basketball games. The committee glosses over the students' comments and charge ahead. Three months into the new Saturday effort the committee is disappointed by the low turnout and ready to give up on reaching students.

This scenario plays out repeatedly in many reservoir congregations. Someone comes up with a good idea and a committee is formed. The committee charges full steam ahead without consulting those they are trying to reach. They are seeking to touch the community but are not leaving space for the community to touch them. Planning to do something in the community without consulting those they seek to reach comes across as paternalistic. It sends the message, "We know what is best for you." Certainly, this is not the intent of the congregation, but it is the result of not allowing the community to touch them.

Reservoir congregations are different from swamp congregations in that they take seriously the call to share the bread of life with the world. They come to the Lord's Table with an understanding that God is calling them to live out what is being given and experienced. Unfortunately, reservoir congregations miss the fact that Communion is about building community together and not dictating the shape it takes. It requires making space for those you seek to be in communion with so they can help shape the community. Let me be clear that I am not suggesting that anything goes. What is shaped together needs to reflect the body of Christ. But a shared vision is more likely to be successful than a dictated one.

In reservoir congregations, we see the importance of sharing the story but also the importance of how that story is shared. The way we invite others into the community matters. Why would someone want to be baptized into a story that they have no part in constructing? To touch others, we must share our story. But to allow others to touch us, we must allow them to become a part of the story.

Canal Churches—A canal congregation is fully living out the story. It is touching the lives of others and allowing others to touch them. Baptism is more than just a ritual. It is the beginning of the journey toward becoming a disciple. The community has structures in place to help everyone entering the community—babies, children, and adults—to begin this journey. For instance, it takes more than a class to learn to practice stewardship by committing prayers, presence, gifts, service, and witness. It is an ongoing process no matter where you are on your spiritual journey.

Communion in canal congregations deepens the way an individual is being formed to share their gifts with God and neighbor. Living out Communion means being invitational in the same way we invite all to God's Table. It means we come to God's Table not simply because we are in the habit of doing so, but because we are truly opening ourselves to God. We come with the expectation that God will touch us.

Returning to my example of a congregation starting a college ministry, a canal congregation would start by inviting college students from the congregation and students not yet a part of the congregation to help shape the ministry. In this way, they are seeking to touch the lives of the students but are also open to the students touching them. Certainly, this is more work with no guarantee of success. But it is a more relational approach that moves beyond a swamp and reservoir mentality.

Canal congregations truly embody the story of Communion by giving themselves away to others in order to bring others around the table. Canal congregations continually seek to "draw the circle wide"—an image made popular by the hymn of the same name by Gordon Light and Mark Miller. The work of expanding community is always challenging, but canal congregations understand this is their calling.

Innovative

Through the prophet Jeremiah, God reveals that something new is going to take place. God is making a new covenant. The old covenant was created to establish Israel as a nation. The laws were given to Moses on stone tablets. The new covenant will be written in the minds and hearts of God's people (Jer 31:31-33).

The new covenant is an innovation on the old covenant. It is created in a way that maintains boundaries and order but allows a certain freedom since it is not literally written in stone. Innovation is not simply doing away with everything that has come before it. Innovation creates space for a new thing to take place by lifting some of the confining characteristics of what has gone before, while continuing to stay in alignment with the same purpose or mission.

In Jeremiah 31, God reveals that the old covenant is going away and a new one is coming. The new covenant is still about God's laws. The expectation is that everyone will embody these laws in new ways and not just see them as words written on stone. The point of innovation is not just to do something new but to do something new that moves toward a positive change. When he healed on the Sabbath, Jesus offered an innovative interpretation of the law, one that would benefit the community, while the temple leaders who challenged him still saw the law as written in stone.

Swamp Churches—Swamp congregations struggle to innovate because they operate as if everything is written in stone. For example, imagine a congregation having a conversation about moving the family Christmas Eve service to the community center down the street. The traditional service would stay at the church, but moving the family service might connect with more families. A backlash develops. What if another family shows up? How will it impact the two families currently attending the church? A swamp congregation is so inwardly focused it cannot innovate because it feels like the things it holds dear will be taken away. These congregations cannot seek to be fully alive because they exist simply for the sake of survival. Hunkering down and settling for mere existence is not the way to be fully alive.

Swamp congregations often avoid innovation because it feels like drastic change. Although innovation does, in most cases, require change, change is not necessarily a negative. Swamp congregations fail to see that it is possible for innovation to maintain the purpose while making life more vital in some fashion. For example, the ability to ride an escalator and not walk up a long staircase is for most people a positive innovation. But it is an innovation that serves the same purpose—moving people from one place to another.

Reservoir Churches—Reservoir congregations do a little better at innovation. They understand that you cannot simply hunker down and expect others to find you. For example, a reservoir congregation would likely not have an issue with the idea of moving the family Christmas Eve service to the community center. In fact, it may even embrace the move and think about cookies and other things to share with the families who come.

The hitch is that the reservoir congregation is going to plan the service without the input of anyone connected to the community center. The service may be exceptional, touching those who come. The problem is those attending do not have an opportunity to return the touch. Being innovative is important, but innovation should include input from those with whom you seek to be in relationship. Your innovative ideas may get people to events, but they will treat the events like an attraction that you visit until the next attraction comes along, unless you seek their input and focus on building relationships.

Reservoir congregations must do new things. But they cannot fall into the trap of planning more events that are merely attractional. They need to include others in developing the new idea so they will feel a part of what is taking place. To some extent, being innovative is the easy part. The challenge is being innovative in a way that helps to build relationships with others and makes the community as a whole better.

Canal Churches—Canal congregations understand the importance of innovation. Canal congregations are looking for ways to do new things that will have positive impact. There is a willingness to think outside of the box and experiment with new approaches. It does not mean everything works, but individuals are invited to think and act on "What if we...?" without fear of getting shut down.

A canal congregation embraces the idea of moving the family Christmas Eve service, and it then looks to partner with individuals at the community center to develop the service. The goal is not simply to take what was done at the church and transplant it to the community center. The goal is to share the Christmas story with the families who come in a manner that connects with them. Perhaps the service takes the form of a play or production that allows the children to participate but without a lot of preparation. Canal congregations understand the need for doing new things in a manner that includes voices beyond the congregation.

Canal congregations are also more innovative because they are willing to fail. Canal congregations are not hung up on things having to turn out perfect. This frees them to try new things without the fear of hearing, "I told you it was a bad idea" or "We tried that before and it didn't work." Innovation is perceived as a way of further participating in God's transforming work and not a burden that detracts from everything the congregation holds dear.

Visionary

The book of Habakkuk is helpful when thinking about visioning. Habakkuk questioned God about the dire circumstances of his people. "And then God answered: Write this. Write what you see. Write it out in big block letters so that it can be read on the run. This vision-message is a witness pointing to what's coming. It aches for the coming—it can hardly wait! And it doesn't lie. If it seems slow in coming, wait. It's on its way. It will come right on time" (Hab 2:2-3 MSG). Imagine seeing hopes and dreams about how your congregation can participate in God's work of transformation written in big block letters so you cannot miss it, no matter where you may be!

The truth is, most congregations have a vision. But is it a vision that pulls them toward the future God is bringing to fruition? Is that vision filed away in a desk drawer and rarely mentioned unless someone happens to bring it up? Congregations must always live in the tension between where they are in the present and where they need to be in the future. Unfortunately, too many churches are satisfied with where they are and have no vision for where they need to be in the future. A vision that truly points toward God's future requires more than lip service.

Swamp Churches—Swamp congregations are satisfied with the status quo. Certainly, these congregations are not writing in big block letters, "We want to stay just as we are!" But what they say and do has the same effect. Swamp congregations talk about what they used to be and avoid conversations about what they can become. The latter requires a vision for moving forward in a way that alters the congregation's story. In many cases, it is not that they cannot embody a different story, but they choose not to.

Imagine a congregation that thrived as the family church. It was known in the community as the family church. But in recent years, only three or four families have been attending. The church is still living out the narrative of being a family church, yet it no longer has a thriving children's ministry or nursery. A developer builds a new apartment complex within walking distance of the church where young and mostly single twenty-something and thirtysomething adults are renting. Instead of reimagining its story to reach young singles, the church continues to have a vision of being the family church. It is not that young single neighbors are opposed to family, but they cannot picture themselves in the church's story.

Swamp congregations struggle because they are unwilling to alter their story even when it is time to do so. The vision never moves beyond what the church is now or what it used to be. Often these congregations believe they are honoring current members and being faithful to the past by preserving their story instead of seeking to live into God's future.

Reservoir Churches—Reservoir congregations have a vision for the future. Reservoir congregations know that simply maintaining the status quo will lead to death. They want others to join them in doing God's work. These congregations construct visions around reaching people and doing things for the community. Reservoir congregations are committed to the present but have an eye on the future as it relates to the church moving forward.

Returning to the example of a congregation that sees itself as a family church, a reservoir congregation finds ways to adapt that story to carry it forward. For example, it reframes the story to reach out to the twenty- and thirty-somethings in the new apartments by saying, "We are a church where you can be a part of our diverse, intergenerational family." Reservoir congregations are willing to alter their story when it ceases to be a compelling vision. But the focus of the story is still the church. These congregations are unwilling to embrace a narrative that does not center around themselves. The vision must still fit inside the box of who they want to be.

Reservoir congregations have an opportunity for moving toward a new future. When they adapt their stories, they may move outside of the box in ways they never imagined. But these congregations can fall back to swamp congregations if the adapted vision fails. The tendency is to become inwardly focused and not to think about other ways of adapting. Because reservoir congregations focus on doing things *for* people, they are vulnerable when individuals outside the church reject their narrative. Reservoir congregations have to work hard at keeping current members engaged in ways that allow them to adapt their story for the future.

Canal Churches—Canal congregations have a vison for the future that requires discerning where God is leading them. It is not that swamp and reservoir congregations are not discerning, but that canal congregations are more willing to alter their story to follow where God is leading. This requires recognizing the importance of helping individuals on their faith journey right now but also having an eye toward where God will lead the congregation next, even if it is a 180-degree change. The truth is, most congregations are unwilling to alter their story significantly because they will feel displaced. Canal congregations believe others can enrich their story in a way that helps them participate more fully in God's transforming work.

Continuing the example of the congregation that was known as the family church, a canal congregation is willing to let go of that story and adopt a new story. For example, the new story may focus on finding community with others who are seeking a place to belong. Certainly, this new story is not a complete departure from the idea of family, but it is not focused on maintaining the family theme. The goal is to develop a story that connects with those in the community who you are seeking to reach. It is important to involve those in the community as you construct a new story. Deciding how to move forward cannot simply be determined in a church committee room. It must emerge from conversations with people in the community.

Canal congregations are truly seeking to be connectors in the way they live out the gospel. Their vision reflects this commitment to connecting with those inside and outside of the church. The challenge for canal congregations arises when they cease to connect with those outside of the congregation and settle for making decisions based on their own preferences. Canal congregations must work hard to fully engage insiders and outsiders at all times as they seek to live out the vison of participating in God's transforming work.

Between a Rock and a Hard Place

Whether a congregation is a swamp, a reservoir, or a canal shapes the way it takes on the missional characteristics of being contextual, communal, innovative, and visionary. All these types of congregations can feel they are stuck between a rock and a hard place. A swamp congregation feels caught between closing its doors or giving up its identity. Neither seems like a good choice. A canal congregation feels the pressure of constantly trying to live into God's vision or receding toward becoming inwardly focused. And neither seems like a good choice.

Part of this tension is that a congregation never has the luxury of resting in place. Congregations are constantly having to think about how they can continue to move positively into the future instead of receding in a negative direction. For congregational leaders, this constant need to move forward for fear of falling backward can feel overwhelming. For leaders in swamp and reservoir congregations, just getting beyond the status quo seems overwhelming and hopeless. They need practical first steps to help their congregations become more missional. Here are a few questions to help a congregation figure out where it falls and needs to move.

Swamp

What is the story the congregation believes about itself? What is the story outsiders believe about the congregation?

Who is the congregation seeking to touch beyond the church?

Are we willing to do anything differently? If yes, what? If no, is it time for us to close?

Reservoir

What is the story the congregation believes about itself? What is the story outsiders believe about the congregation?

How are we allowing others to touch us beyond the church?

Are we willing to change our story to connect with others? If yes, how? If no, are we willing to move toward a swamp mentality?

Canal

What is the story the congregation believes about itself? What is the story outsiders believe about the congregation?

Are we becoming complacent in the way we touch lives and they touch our lives?

Are we continuing to discern where God is leading us?
If yes, how? If no, are we willing to move toward a reservoir mentality?

These questions are a way of entering into a discussion around being missional. I am not suggesting every congregation should be or can be a canal congregation. But I do believe we need more reservoir congregations. We need more congregations that are not hunkering down and just living out their time, congregations that are truly committed to participating in God's transforming work. It is true that congregations cannot escape being stuck between a rock and a hard place, but they can decide a missional way of moving forward.

ESTHER INTERLUDE FOUR

When Esther's words were reported to Mordecai, he sent back this answer: "Do not think that because you are in the king's house you alone of all the Jews will escape. For if you remain silent at this time, relief and deliverance for the Jews will arise from another place, but you and your father's family will perish. And who knows but that you have come to your royal position for such a time as this?"

—Esther 4:12-14

In response to Mordecai's warning, Esther experiences a transformation. She moves from just going along with her cousin to setting her own agenda. At the beginning of the chapter, Esther knows her cousin is troubled and she wants to help. She seeks to help Mordecai without having to think outside established patterns. She sends Mordecai clothes rather than addressing the underlying issue. Then his words clarify the urgency and the opportunity; she can see herself as an essential part of God's plan for her community. Her thinking moves from the customary and safe to the creative and bold.

Similarly, congregations often want to address problems without thinking beyond established patterns. They seek easy solutions rather than dealing with more serious underlying issues. Few youth are connecting with a congregation even though the neighborhood is full of young people. The congregation's first response is to post a picture on the church website of the two youth who do come to church under the banner headline, "All youth are welcome!" This solution doesn't require any transformation. It doesn't require that the church do anything new or different.

Like Esther, congregations easily fall into the pattern of solving problems without having to think outside of the box. They buy into quick fixes that maintain the status quo. Things continue as they are. Disrupting the status quo is hard and takes more work than we imagine. Consciously or unconsciously, most of us are comfortable with things the way they are.

If we are honest with ourselves, many of us want nondisruptive transformation. We are fine with some things being different if all the things we like about the status quo remain the same. The youth are welcome to come *as long as* it does not disrupt the way we worship. The children can come *as long as* the parents keep them quiet during church. You fill in the blank: "_____ *as long as* _____." The point is, many of us like the idea of transformation *as long as* what we like continues to be the same.

Mordecai's famous words to Esther, "for such a time as this," are powerful because they invite her to consider different possibilities. Yes, Mordecai speaks these words from a position of relative safety. But this phrase opens new possibilities for moving beyond the status quo into uncharted territory. It moves beyond the "as long as" way of approaching transformation.

Many congregations today are facing their "for such a time as this" moment. Will they decide to be disruptive and move forward into uncharted territory? Or will they let the moment slip by and stick with the relative comfort of the status quo? Esther ultimately chooses disruption and makes plans to move forward boldly. The next chapter considers how we can be similarly bold as we navigate uncharted territory. It is risky, of course. We know Esther's gamble paid off, but we do not have the benefit of knowing the ending of our own stories. Yet, at the same time, it can be liberating to break free of the constraints of the status quo, even if they are comfortable. There is something biblical about stepping out in faith!

Chapter Five

NAVIGATING

If the goal for all Christian communities is to participate in God's transforming work, what is the process for doing this? How do swamp and reservoir congregations take the next faithful step? The key is to continually ask, "How do we as a congregation participate in God's transforming work?" And the key to answering this question involves the congregation's mission and vision. How do they align with efforts to participate in God's transforming work?

Adept congregations are best suited to take the next faithful step. But all congregations—even adept congregations—need to overcome obstacles to move forward. The more swamp characteristics a congregation has, the greater the obstacles. Even canal congregations confront things blocking them from even greater participation in God's work.

Many times, as I am driving to or from work, something blocks my intended route. If I'm smart, I check traffic before I leave so I can anticipate potential blockers. But sometimes, even the best planning goes out the window because an accident occurs right in front of me, causing a blockage. It's no different for a church trying to take the next faithful step. Blockages can get in the way of even adept churches. They have set a good path, but blockers start to get in the way.

How can we recognize things that might block progress in order to better navigate around them? Any number of things could be blockers, but five common types of obstacles are those involving *conduct, communication, commitment, conflict,* and *complacency.* Problems in these areas can stall the momentum gained as a congregation becomes more adept at decision making and having the right influence.

What is unique and most challenging about these types of blockers is that they can be forms of self-sabotage—ways we block our own efforts to move forward. It's bad enough to stumble over blocks that others place in front of us, but dealing with stumbling blocks we set ourselves is even more challenging. Internal blockers are things we do to ourselves that prevent us from flourishing.

Conduct

In Exodus, we read the story of how God forms the Israelites into a nation as they wander through the wilderness. The people grumble against Moses and God. Finally, it gets to a point where God decides that those beyond the age of twenty will not see the Promised Land because of their unseemly conduct, except for Caleb and Joshua, who "followed the LORD wholeheartedly" (Num 32:11-12). These older generations were formed in slavery in Egypt and could not completely escape that orientation. Even when they were free, they still behaved as if they were in bondage. They exhibit certain negative conduct toward God and Moses whenever anything goes wrong. They complain that there is no food. When God provides manna from heaven, they complain that all there is to eat is manna. Their complaints all end with the same refrain: "Were we not better off in slavery in Egypt?" In Egypt, the Israelites had become conditioned to expect certain things and act in certain ways. Being free in the desert is disorienting to them. It disrupts their normal patterns of expectations and actions. They conduct themselves in negative ways because they could not reorient themselves to a new environment that requires different expectations and actions.

Such behavior in the face of a dramatic change in circumstance is not unique to the Israelites. Picture a congregation that was vibrant during the late 1950s and 1960s but struggles now with fewer people and fewer resources. More than half a century later, the congregation still behaves like it's the 1960s. Like the Israelites in the desert, the congregation conducts itself in negative and unhelpful ways because it holds on to expectations and actions formed in a different era. This type of conduct can block a church from participating in God's transformation. A church grumbling, "Were we not better off in Egypt?" blocks the process of transformation. When God sends manna from heaven, the church asks, "Is this all there is?" Like the Israelites, the church is probably not intentionally blocking transformation. It may be unaware of how conduct shaped in other times or circumstances keeps them from leaving Egypt—physically, spiritually, and mentally. The way a church conducts itself can be a powerful blocker preventing it from moving forward.

Communication

Progress can be stalled by blocks in communication. Naaman, the commander of the Aramean army that defeated Israel, had leprosy. A girl who was captured in the war and given to Naaman's wife tells his wife that Elisha could cure leprosy. Naaman tells the Aramean king what the girl told his wife. The

Aramean king gives Naaman a letter to give to the king of Israel, asking the king—not Elisha—to cure Naaman. The king of Israel despairs because the Aramean king has sent his army commander to ask the impossible, which he thinks must be a pretext for more war. Elisha sends word to the despairing king to send Naaman to him. But when Naaman arrives with horses and chariots at Elisha's gate, all he gets is a message with Elisha's prescription to bathe in a local river. Naaman is so aggravated that he would have left then and there if his servants had not convinced him to follow the prophet's order. Naaman bathed in the Jordan seven times and was healed and, from then on, worshipped the Lord (2 Kgs 5:1-19).

How many times do we ignore clear communication in our congregations? We are excited about starting a ministry to connect better with our neighbors. It is communicated to us that changing the day of the week will be helpful in connecting with more people. But we ignore what is communicated because we have our own preconceptions about how it will work. Sometimes it is hard for us to hear simple truths or suggestions.

Naaman ignores the simple suggestion at first because it does not meet his expectations. We do the same in congregations when new plans don't meet our expectations. Naaman eventually goes to the Jordan after his servants convince him he has nothing to lose. But unfortunately, too many congregations get blocked because they never get beyond ignoring the simple truths. How we interpret and act on what is being communicated plays a big role in every organization. Sometimes we get blocked because of poor communication. But sometimes we get blocked because we ignore straightforward communication.

Commitment

When something new starts, people often get excited and jump on board. But six months down the road, the initial excitement is wearing off, and some people stop participating as often as they did at first. A year down the road, even more people are dropping off. And this continues over time. Waning enthusiasm is one of the most challenging blockers for congregations. There is a lot of excitement and participation when a new Bible study first starts, but as the weeks go by, the commitment starts to dwindle.

Most people want their church to thrive and will step up to the plate to help. But as the commitment level wanes, it is hard to sustain a long-term change process. And the truth is, a long-term commitment is required if a swamp congregation is to become a reservoir. It may be possible to get people excited to show up on a Saturday to connect with neighbors. Getting them to show up the first Saturday of each month for a year is a challenge.

I imagine that the Israelites were excited when they left Egypt. They were probably thinking, "Finally, we are free!" Then they get out in the wilderness and their commitment to freedom starts to diminish. The idea of freedom sounded great, but the actual work of being free is a much bigger commitment than they had imagined. Like the Israelites, we like the idea of something new and different, like connecting with our neighbors. But rarely do we consider the level of commitment it takes to stick with something new over the long haul. We block ourselves by not fully committing to the practices that can transform our congregation. We like the idea of transformation but not the commitment required to carry it out.

Conflict

Sometimes, ego gets in the way. For example, James and John, the sons of Zebedee, asked Jesus to seat them at his right and left hand in glory. Although all the disciples had healed, taught, and fed the multitudes, the two that Jesus nicknamed Sons of Thunder, together with Peter, witnessed the raising of the daughter of Jairus, the transfiguration, and the arrest of Jesus. In pressing Jesus to promise them a special status, the brothers said they comprehended the cross and the triumph over it, but they failed to grasp the mission. Their play for special consideration made the other disciples indignant, giving Jesus reason to remind all of them that "whoever wants to become great among you must be your servant" (Mark 10:35-45).

The same thing can happen in our churches. For example, a new Wednesday night mentoring program for middle schoolers really starts to take off. Everyone is excited about the connections being made with the youth and the families. Then one participant goes to the pastor and says, "I think I should be the director of the program since I have been at the church the longest." Word gets back to the other participants and they are not pleased. In fact, they are indignant!

James and John caused a conflict when self-promotion diverted them from the mission they were called to serve. The mentor at the church does the same. We expect conflict when things are going poorly, but it catches us off guard when things are going well. Unexpected conflict can be twice as bad because individuals feel they have been betrayed. In many cases, the conflict centers around who has power or authority. Jesus answered James and John by saying, "to sit at my right hand or at my left is not mine to grant" (Mark 10:40 NRSV). Unfortunately, we cannot use Jesus's answer. But we need to be aware of power dynamics that can cause conflict and derail a good work taking place.

Complacency

Complacency is another potential blocker when we start experiencing transformation. We think, "We've made it! We are finally secure." Imagine someone who grew up in a working-class family and worked her way through college. She gets a good job and moves into the neighborhood and house of her dreams. But she is lulled into complacency, thinking she is finally secure and without worries. She loses her job and realizes how quickly things can change.

A church can also become complacent. It starts doing the things required to become adept and missionally-focused. Soon, it starts to believe that its financial crisis is over. It has finally turned the corner and is no longer at risk of closing. But when it starts to think it is finally secure, it is at risk of becoming complacent.

The prophet Amos warns, "Alas for those who are at ease in Zion, and for those who feel secure on Mount Samaria" (Amos 6:1 NRSV). It is a warning not to be satisfied with the status quo. Complacency is a powerful blocker because when our hard work begins to bear fruit, we become satisfied. We become complacent in Zion, thinking nothing can touch us. It is at that moment that things can begin falling apart. We believe the crisis is over, so we no longer keep pushing. We fall back into old patterns. Complacency is a dangerous blocker because it can sneak up on you. You think you have finally turned the corner only to find out that you are taking two steps backward. We have to keep a watchful eye out for the signs of complacency. There is nothing more frustrating than experiencing a taste of transformation only to fall back into the same old habits.

There are any number of other blockers that can derail a church's momentum. But the roadblocks described above are particularly troubling because we often set them ourselves. It is one thing to learn to navigate around obstacles others have set in your path. But we are often blind to the obstacles we create ourselves. To maneuver successfully around these potential traps, a church needs to be attentive to the ways conduct, communication, commitment, conflict, and complacency can catch it off guard. Adept churches stay on the path by looking ahead for the problems that could knock it off course.

Navigate

A good driver learns to navigate in all kinds of circumstances. When the road is clear. When the road is wet. When the road is covered with snow. When tree branches are in the middle of the road. You get the point. A good driver makes adjustments along the way as circumstances warrant. The challenge is making the right adjustments.

Congregations must make the right adjustments to maneuver around external and internal blockers while trying to navigate toward God's future. The right adjustments keep a congregation on the path to flourishing. There's no magic formula for making the right adjustments, but some things have a better chance of success.

People Express Airlines was a discount air carrier based in Newark, New Jersey, that began operating in 1981. Innovative practices allowed People Express to undercut more established airlines on certain key routes. This new discount carrier charged the same fare for almost every seat on the plane. They charged baggage fees if a passenger had more than one bag. And they charged for snacks and sodas as well. When People Express first entered the market, their flights were sold out and things were going well. But their competitors caught on relatively quickly and lowered their fares, and the new discount airline could not adjust to counter this move. By 1987 People Express could no longer sustain its business model and merged with Continental Airlines.

There are many similar stories. An adept organization tries something new and it takes off. It seems to be working and they are on a path toward flourishing. But eventually, what worked initially no longer works as well. And the inability to adjust course prevents continued success. Many congregations have blazed a path of success, but like People Express their success is curtailed by an inability to adjust to setbacks.

It takes courage to adjust a seemingly successful plan. Courage? Really? We think of courage as a virtue on the battlefield, not in the realm of congregational life. But it takes courage to confront things that frighten us and prevent us from acting. In some cases, courage amounts to doing something others see as foolish. For example, when Paul and Silas are jailed in Philippi, an earthquake causes the jail doors to fly open. The jailor sensibly assumes they have escaped. If you were wrongly imprisoned away from home and the jail doors flew open, would you stick around? But Paul and Silas demonstrate courage by staying put and not leaving, saving the jailor from shame and converting him to Christianity (Acts 16:25-34).

Courage is not screaming loudly and running full speed at your opponents, as we see on TV and in the movies. For one congregation, courage is partnering with the church across the street that is of a different ethnicity, despite a long history of troubled relations. To stay on course, this congregation must be courageous enough to confront its own history and partner with individuals who are suspicious of their motives. For another congregation, courage is supporting those without voice in the church who have been bullied for years by one of the church's top financial givers. This church has to adjust its thinking to create an inclusive community where all have voice, regardless of whether they are rich or poor. Not every adjustment is as dramatic as these examples. But they illustrate the way courage works when we are faced with having to adjust our plans.

In most instances, the easy choice is to maintain the status quo. It takes courage to navigate in a different direction. Courageous congregations are better able to make difficult adjustments. Those without courage may start off on the right path, but progress is stymied because they, like People Express, cannot make midcourse corrections. Adept congregations are courageous enough to overcome blockers and change course.

Making challenging adjustments also requires creativity. When confronted by a challenge, we often try to resolve it by doing what we have done in the past—even when we don't realize it. If I have an older car that keeps breaking down, I may fix it myself or finally take it to a mechanic. If I don't like that mechanic's advice, I may take it to another mechanic. The point is, I keep trying to resolve the issue by fixing the old car. I never stop to think whether it would be more prudent to put the money I am spending to fix an old car toward the purchase of a new car. It's hard to think outside the box. Our solutions stay inside the box because the parameters of the box define how we see things.

Have you ever heard the story of a truck stuck under a bridge? The truck driver can't figure out how to get the truck out from under the bridge. The police can't figure out how to get the truck out. The fire department can't think of a way to get the truck out. The county engineers figure the best plan is to cut away a part of the bridge, which would be costly and time consuming. A young girl walking with her mom says out loud, "Why don't they just flatten the tires?" All the experts grin sheepishly. They never considered that option. When our thinking stays within a box, that box shapes how we see our options.

How can a congregation think outside the box? We typically get trapped inside the box when the same individuals are analyzing the same information. They have been trained to see things in a certain way. Getting a fresh perspective can help. The fresh perspective can come from someone at another church or, even better, someone from the community. Someone with a different perspective will not be trapped by the same assumptions that unconsciously keep us thinking within the box.

We also get trapped inside the box when we limit what we think is possible to what we think is financially viable. This does not mean we should ignore financial implications, because funds are limited in most congregations. But finances should not be the starting point. When looking at a new possibility or making course adjustments, we need to avoid looking first through the lens of money and finances. When every great idea has to fit within certain financial parameters, our thinking stays in the box.

We can get trapped inside the box when we limit our plans based on our current knowledge and capacity. For example, developing an app may help us to reach more people in the community. But we nix the idea because we do not know how to develop apps. Perhaps the app could be developed through a partnership or by finding the right expert. Limiting possibilities up front by failing to think beyond your current capacity keeps your thinking inside the box.

Creativity does not always require that we come up with a solution that has never been thought of before. But it does require that we get outside the box and open ourselves to new ways of seeing and doing. No matter the size of your congregation, you can always get a fresh perspective. You can avoid starting every conversation with the subject of money. And you can explore ideas that are beyond your existing knowledge and capacity. These three ways of getting outside the box will help your congregation become more creative when it has to adjust course.

Adjusters

If adept congregations must learn to adjust course, their leaders need to be adept at being *adjusters*. By that I mean people who can keep us moving forward when our path is blocked. In most cases, these individuals will not see themselves as adjusters. They probably think of themselves as can-do people who like the challenge of creative problem solving. Pay attention to this type of person. They may play the essential role of adjuster on your team.

Leaders with this ability are not necessarily the visionaries, but they understand the vision and can make shifts when progress toward the vision stalls. No matter how good the vision and mission, adjustments will have to be made along the way. Adjusters carve a path forward in a way that maintains the integrity of what the congregation is seeking to do.

More than one person can take on the critical role of adjuster. Depending on the circumstances, Shelia might be the right person in one case, and James the right person in another case.

A congregation on the path to becoming adept must learn to navigate successfully. This includes making adjustments to get around the things blocking your path. These adjustments often require creativity and courage. Who are the adjusters in your church who can lead the changes in course necessary to keep your congregation moving forward?

Between a Rock and a Hard Place

The work of navigating a congregation is challenging. This is true even when things are going well. Trying to keep the congregation moving forward and not falling back into an abyss feels like navigating between a rock and a hard place. The challenge is trying to move forward into a new and unfamiliar space without falling back into a familiar space that is becoming more and more like a swamp. Here are some questions to consider as you work to navigate your congregation forward.

What are the external blockers in your path?

What are the internal blockers in your path? (Use the list in this chapter as a starting point.)

What are the things you are afraid to confront in making adjustments needed to move forward?

What parameters are you setting in trying to make adjustments needed to move forward?

Who are those individuals in your congregation who are best suited to be adjusters?

Answering these questions will get you started on navigating in a more helpful way.

CONCLUSION

*When Esther's words were reported to Mordecai, he sent back
this answer: "Do not think that because you are in the king's
house you alone of all the Jews will escape. For if you remain
silent at this time, relief and deliverance for the Jews will arise
from another place, but you and your father's family will perish.
And who knows but that you have come to your royal position
for such a time as this?"*

—Esther 4:12-14

At the end of chapter 4, Esther figures out she must navigate adeptly between a rock and a hard place—between
her possible demise and the demise of her people. There is no
easy way forward. Either choice could have devastating results.
Far too many congregations are in the same boat as Esther. They
are navigating between a rock and a hard place—between the
possibility of having to close their doors and an uncertain future
going in a direction they have never imagined. There is no easy
way forward. Either choice could have devastating results.

Most congregations struggle to confront honestly their own
circumstance. Are they a swamp, a reservoir, or a canal? These
congregations are stuck between falling further in the abyss or
moving toward deeper missional engagement. The challenge
is most daunting for swamp congregations who are closest to

death but still have the possibility of becoming a reservoir. While not every congregation can advance to the point of being a canal, every congregation can embrace the goal of becoming more missional.

The first step is to focus on just one ministry. Whether your congregation is a swamp, reservoir, or canal, how can you strengthen one program or ministry area? So often we try to run before we can walk or even crawl. We all need to start with baby steps. Then, as we develop and gain experience, we become more adept at moving forward. If a swamp congregation can successfully transform one ministry, it can develop a new way of being. But it is critical to make adept decisions and cultivate the right kind of influence all along the way.

Take time to reflect deliberately on the steps necessary for your congregation to become more adept. These five things can help get you started down the right path.

1. Have a group of key leaders and potential leaders read this book.

The group does not need to be large. Where two or three are gathered, Jesus is in their midst. But these two or three should be individuals who can journey with you toward a deeper missional engagement. The goal is to ascertain who from this group is willing to do the work of becoming adept. Individual leaders will come and go. But regardless of the gifts of individual leaders, they must learn to be adept if the congregation is going to thrive.

2. Name the reality of your church.

Is your church a swamp, a reservoir, or a canal? There is no need to assign blame or dredge up old warts from the past. But honesty is essential to moving forward. Many congregations are held back by their inability to see truthfully who they really are. They think they are hospitable and outwardly focused when the truth is, they are hospitable only to people they know, and they are outwardly focused only at Christmastime. The goal is not shaming, but an honest starting point.

3. Focus on becoming adept.

Analyze the way decisions are adopted and adapted in your church. Think about the way influence is used. Your leadership group needs to learn to think differently about the way decisions are made and how influence is used in decision making. Start with one ministry. Don't try to do everything at once.

4. Name your fears and acknowledge the parameters around you.

This will help the group anticipate where they may encounter blockers and figure out how to get out of the box. We often fail to move forward because we don't anticipate internal roadblocks and how they force us back into the box. To do a new thing, you must to be deliberate about getting outside the box.

5. Determine the leaders best able to make the right adjustments.

No matter how well we plan, adjustments will be needed along the way. To stay on a path to success, you need to find the right people who can help you to make the necessary adjustments as you go forward. Keep your eyes open. These right people may not be a part of your current leadership group.

The biblical story of Esther is a helpful analogy, but the analogy only goes so far. Esther's story concludes with a happy ending. For congregations, the work never ends until Jesus returns. In a sense, congregations will always be between a rock and a hard place. Our constant challenge is to navigate and adjust to keep moving forward missionally. Our challenge is ongoing in a way that Esther's challenge was not.

But I am confident that all congregations can become more adept as they navigate between a rock and a hard place. Realistically, I know not every congregation will end up as a canal. But many swamp congregations can take the next faithful step and become a reservoir. Just think of the difference it will make in our communities if there are many more reservoir congregations. I truly believe we are called to this work for such a time as this!

NOTES

Introduction

1. Michael Lipka, "A Closer Look at America's Rapidly Growing Religious 'Nones,'" *Fact Tank*, Pew Research Center, May 13, 2015, www.pewresearch.org/fact-tank/2015/05/13/a -closer-look-at-americas-rapidly-growing-religious-nones/.

1. Swamp, Reservoir, or Canal

1. Howard Thurman, *Mediations of the Heart* (New York: Harper and Brothers Publishers, 1953), 86.
2. Thurman, *Mediations of the Heart*, 87.
3. Thurman, *Mediations of the Heart*, 87.
4. Thurman, *Mediations of the Heart*, 87.
5. Thurman, *Mediations of the Heart*, 86.
6. Thurman, *Mediations of the Heart*, 87.
7. Thurman, *Mediations of the Heart*, 86.
8. Thurman, *Mediations of the Heart*, 86.

2. Adept Congregation

1. I am not referring to the adaptive leadership model introduced by Ron Heifetz and Marty Linsky.

3. Influence

1. Tom Berlin and Lovett H. Weems, Jr., *High Yield: Seven Disciplines of the Fruitful Leader* (Nashville: Abingdon Press, 2014), 86.

CPSIA information can be obtained
at www.ICGtesting.com
Printed in the USA
LVHW040317210220
647687LV00006B/7